SWEETY PIES

An Uncommon Collection of Womanish Observations, *with Pie*

PATTY PINNER

PHOTOGRAPHS BY ALEXANDRA GRABLEWSKI

The Taunton Press

For Mama, who used to tell me,
"Good cooking involves more than just stirring in the pots."

The Taunton Press, Inc., 63 South Main Street, PO Box 5506, Newtown, CT 06470-5506
e-mail: tp@taunton.com

Editor: Pamela Hoenig
Interior design: Alison Wilkes
Layout: Amy Russo, Kimberly Shake
Photographer: Alexandra Grablewski (cover and food photography)

Library of Congress Cataloging-in-Publication Data
Pinner, Patty, 1954-
Sweety pies : an uncommon collection of womanish observations, with pie / Patty Pinner.
p. cm.
Includes bibliographical references and index.
ISBN-13: 978-1-56158-848-0
ISBN-13: 978-1-60085-035-6 Special Edition
1. Pies. I. Title.

TX773.P5747 2007
641.8'652--dc22

2007001789

Printed in Singapore
10 9 8 7 6 5 4 3 2 1

Acknowledgments

I'M SO GRATEFUL To my aunts, Marjell, Helen, and Betty Jean who continue to share their wonderful recipes with me, and encourage my best womanish cooking To my cousin, Michelle Thompson, one of the few people I can call when I want to talk recipes and girl talk at the same time To Nora Dawkins and Minelva Allen, whose friendship and late-night womanly conversations sharpen my insight and show me the way To my friend Pamela Wyrick, who early on encouraged me to share my recipes and tell my stories. Pam, you have been a blessing in my life—I owe you so much To Reitus Wilson, Jocelyn Gordon, Susan Clark, Althea Hatter, Debra Defoe, Judy Sommer, Lisa Kamrad, and Annabelle Deniozos for their support. I love you dearly–you are all bona fide sweety pies

And, if the truth be told, I know a few men who are real sweety pies too, supplying me with love and support, whenever I need it. I especially want to thank: My cousins Ryan Sims, Larry Moore, and Jeffrey Thompson for always looking out for me Thomas Gillespie, Bradford Nutt, William Ketchum, Vernon Beasley, and Gregory Woods; thank you for your generous love—because of your example, I speak up whenever I hear women lumping all men together Dante Toussaint; thank you so much for bringing music back into my life.

And, I *really* want to thank: My editor, Pamela Hoenig, and the people working with her at Taunton Press, for bringing this lovely book to market. Thank you, Pam, for editing, rearranging chapters, and guiding me through Jane Falla, of the Lisa Ekus Public Relations Company, for her words of wisdom and encouragement. Jane, our conversations lift me up every time we speak And last, Lisa Ekus, who absolutely changed my life a few years ago, when she answered my query with, "Sure; send it in. I'd love to read your manuscript." A heartfelt thanks to you, Lisa, for being my mentor and friend.

Contents

Introduction

I made my first pie when I was three years old. To me, the pie was a beautiful little confection that symbolized all good things, because, even then, I was careful to heed the ancient pie-making admonition that the women in my family held onto: only the finest ingredients will do. My pie was made from the freshest mud and tap water available. And I garnished it with rose petals I had collected from the rosebushes my mother meticulously cultivated. My pie symbolized what all good pies do: love and caring.

In fact, the American dessert pie is the ultimate expression of what comfort food, old-fashioned family values, and wholesome living represent. A homemade fruit pie cooling on a window sill is still the American icon of domestic solace and bliss.

When I was growing up in Saginaw, Michigan, a small, Mayberry-like town 90 miles north of Detroit, no matter how good a woman cooked, the true measure of her cooking prowess was determined by the quality of the pies she passed at family dinners and social gatherings. The crusts had to be flaky and browned just right. The fillings had to be rich, moist, and hold the perfect measure of sweetness.

I am a descendant of that generation where a woman's appearance, manner, and domestic prowess were synonymous with her feminine identity. Back then, feminine seduction was an art that women applied to all the levels of their being, even housekeeping. I can still remember how my mother would light a stick of incense and fluff the living room pillows just before my father came home from work, and how she'd offer him a sample of his dinner—straight from her hands to his waiting mouth. "Does it need anything?" she'd ask, knowing full well that Daddy didn't know a thing about spices.

In our community, a woman who kept a spotless house was given the coveted title: Quite a Homemaker. But a woman whose pies were as beautifully crafted as they were delicious, well, that woman, even though she may have fallen short on a variety of other social graces, was considered a bona fide domestic goddess.

Without question, pies are my favorite dessert. Nothing satisfies my desire for something sweet better than pie. Presented with a choice of fruit or custard, I'd have trouble saying for certain which filling I like best. As long as the crust is tender and flaky, and there's plenty of it, I don't think there's a pie I couldn't learn to love.

In the same way that I enjoy collecting recipes, I take real pleasure in gathering the stories of the women the recipes belong to. I am a firm believer that what a woman cooks is a window into her womanly personality—what she thinks, how she behaves, how she feels about herself and the people she cooks for. In that regard, I believe that every woman has her special recipes and that those recipes are attached to stories that reveal the essence of the woman. You can learn a lot about yourself by studying the essences of other women. Therefore, I offer this volume of recipes and womanish observations in the hope that, after reading them, you will be left with more than just a wonderful collection of pies, but also, every time you light your oven, a heightened sense of the power you have when you are a cooking woman.

1

A Good Pie Crust

"You can't have a good pie if you don't have a good pie crust."

—Ruth Pinner, my mother

When I was growing up, I did not lack for domestic symbols of womanhood. My mother had a passion for collecting recipes; she owned more than 300 cookbooks, which she studied like tomes of womanly magic. (She bought me my first *Betty Crocker Cookbook* when I was eight.) Every Christmas, my grandmother's gift to me had something to do with running a pretty household: one year, a mock kitchen, replete with an Easy-Bake® oven, another year, a set of play dishes and play pots and pans. When I got a little older, she gave me her prized collection of ruffled aprons. Even though my grandmother's gifts were meant for play, we all knew that, through her gifts, she wanted me to master the art of domesticity; I could see in her eyes that she meant them as more than just playthings. My aunts were also members of the same league of domestic artisans that my mother and grandmother belonged to—they, too, believed it was their duty to pass along our family's women's wisdom; in that way, I had many teachers.

When I was a young girl, I loved being in the kitchen with my mother. Mama's kitchen was shrouded in an air of passion and mystery. She told womanly stories in her kitchen, disclosed family secrets in her kitchen, and hid her *ain't-gonna-put-up-with-no-unnecessary-mess-from-no-man* cookie jar savings account in her kitchen. She kept the bottles of her most potent herbs and spices turned around so that you couldn't read their labels. My mother was a jewel of many facets—part diamond, part jade, part ruby, part turquoise. When she was in her kitchen, when she was cooking for her man (my dad), you saw one aspect of her kitchen personality; when she was cooking for company, you saw another.

Growing up with a mother who loved to cook caused me to spend a lot of time in the kitchen. My mother was very candid with me about becoming a woman; the kitchen was where we did most of our talking and, therefore, was the backdrop for most of my earliest recollections. But while I loved sitting in the kitchen talking to my mother and watching her cook, I never wanted to be a real, apron-and-pearls domestic diva. That kind of olden Donna Reed ideology defined my mother, grandmother, and aunts—women from a bygone era, not a modern Cosmo girl like me, who could whip up an entire meal simply by opening a box and mixing its contents with a little tap water.

But a funny thing happened; now that I'm older, I see so many ways in which I am my mother. I see so many ways in which *all* of the women in my family, and many from my community, have left their culinary marks on me. The womanly kitchen skills that once seemed so useless now make sense to me. I finally understand what they were trying to tell me in their kitchen stories: Cooking for a man is as much an art form as painting on a canvas; and a pie crust made from scratch tastes so much better than even the most delectable store-bought kinds.

Mama Used to Say

My mother used to tell me, "You'll know when you've got a good pie because your crust will be crisp and golden and your filling won't be undercooked or overcooked; it'll be set just right." Mama said, sometimes it was necessary to cook the crust and the filling separately, so that when they came together, they would complement each other nicely. Here is a little tenet that she passed on to me: when a pie filling is cooked on top of the stove, like the filling for lemon meringue pie, you should bake your crust completely *before you fill it. When a filling is juicy, the way many fruit fillings are, the bottom crust will hold up if you partially bake it.*

Flaky Pie Crust

9- OR 10-INCH SINGLE CRUST

- 1⅓ cups all-purpose flour
- 1 teaspoon sugar
- ¼ teaspoon salt
- ½ cup chilled vegetable shortening
- 3 tablespoons ice-cold heavy cream or evaporated milk, more or less as needed

9-INCH DOUBLE CRUST OR 9-INCH DEEP-DISH SINGLE CRUST

- 2¼ cups all-purpose flour
- 2 teaspoons sugar
- ½ teaspoon salt
- 1 cup chilled vegetable shortening
- 5 to 6 tablespoons of ice-cold heavy cream or evaporated milk, more or less as needed

The glory of a good pie isn't established solely by the thick, sugary juices that bubble up to the top; the magnificence of a good pie has as much to do with the taste and the texture of the crust as it has to do with the filling.

My mother taught me how to make pie crusts. She used to say, "A woman doesn't have to be a gourmet cook to set a nice table. But there are certain things that every woman who considers herself a decent cook ought to know how to do well; making a crust from scratch is one of them."

This recipe is easy and produces a crust you will be proud to serve.

Sift the flour, sugar, and salt together in a medium-size to large bowl. Using a pastry blender, a big serving fork, or the tips of your fingers, cut in or pinch or squeeze the shortening until the mixture resembles a bowl of sweet peas. Tossing the mixture quickly and lightly with a fork, sprinkle in the cream or milk 1 tablespoon at a time. (It's better to err on the side of not having enough liquid than to have too much; you don't want a soupy crust.) Continue tossing until the dough holds together when lightly pressed.

With lightly floured hands, loosely gather up the dough into a flat ball, place it in a bowl, and cover with plastic wrap. Refrigerate until you are ready to roll out the crust. I try to chill at least 30 minutes but not too much longer than overnight.

Gather together your pie dish, rolling pin, flour canister, flour sifter, and a small, sharp knife. Prepare a clean surface for rolling out the dough. Sift enough flour over the surface to prevent the dough from sticking to it. Lightly flour your hands and the rolling pin. Place the chilled dough on the surface. If you are making a double-crust pie, divide the dough into two balls, one ball (it will be used as the bottom crust) slightly larger than the other (top crust). Keep the top crust covered and refrigerated while you roll out the bottom crust. Press it into a small, flat disk. Using the rolling pin, roll the dough into a circle, working from the center to the edges. Starting at the center, roll straight up to the edge, turn the dough slightly, and roll straight up to the edge. Repeat the process—turning the dough and rolling—until the dough has formed a circle that's slightly larger than the pan. (Make a 12-inch circle for a 9-inch pan, or a 13-inch circle for a 10-inch pan, or a 12 x 16-inch rectangle for a 9 x 13-inch pan.) Be careful to keep the dough as even as you can, about ¼ to ⅛ inch thick.

Place the pie plate upside down on top of the rolled-out dough. Using a small knife, cut a circle around the plate, leaving a 1-inch border of dough around the plate. Set aside the scraps. Remove the pie plate. Gently fold the crust in half. Now, fold the crust into quarters. Gently pick up the crust and place it in the pie plate so the center point of the crust is positioned in the center of the plate. Unfold the dough and press it firmly into position in the plate. Trim all excess dough from the edge, except for a ½-inch flap of dough around the edge.

If you are making a single crust pie, crimp the edge first, then fill with the pie filling. If you are making a double-crust pie, fill the pie, then roll out the second crust the same way you rolled the bottom crust. Cut the top crust so it extends beyond that of the bottom crust. (Cut an 11-inch circle for a 9-inch pie, a 13-inch circle for a 10-inch pie, and a 10 x 14-inch rectangle for a 9 x 13-inch pie.) Place the top crust on top of the filled pie. Trim the overhang to ½ inch. Fold the top flap of dough under the edge of the bottom crust, until the edges are even with the rim of the pan. Using the tines of a fork, flatten the hem evenly against the rim of the pie plate, moving completely around the pie. To prevent sticking, dip the fork in flour, if needed. Cut a few slits on top of the crust to let out the steam, then bake as directed in your particular recipe.

Prebaking a Pie Crust

To partially bake an empty single pie crust, you need to line your pie plate with the crust. Flute the edges of the crust, refrigerate it for 30 minutes, then take it from the refrigerator and line it with parchment or waxed paper. Place pie weights or dried beans on top of the paper so the dough doesn't puff up and rise out of the plate as it bakes. Set the crust in a preheated 425 degree oven and bake until the top edges start to turn light brown, 8 to 10 minutes. Take the crust out of the oven and remove the paper and pie weights. Reduce the oven temperature to 350 degrees, return the crust back in the oven, and bake until the crust just starts to turn golden brown, another 5 minutes. Let it cool completely on a wire rack.

To fully bake the crust, leave it in the oven an additional 3 to 5 minutes, until fully golden brown. Let it cool completely on a wire rack.

9-INCH DEEP-DISH DOUBLE CRUST OR 10-INCH DOUBLE CRUST

- 2½ cups all-purpose flour
- 1 tablespoon sugar
- 1 teaspoon salt
- 1 cup chilled vegetable shortening
- 7 to 8 tablespoons ice-cold heavy cream or evaporated milk, more or less as needed

9 X 13-INCH DOUBLE CRUST

- 4 cups all-purpose flour
- 1½ tablespoons granulated sugar
- 1 teaspoon salt
- 2 cups chilled vegetable shortening
- ½ cup ice-cold heavy cream or evaporated milk, more or less as needed

Adding a Special Touch

Once when I was a little girl, my mother called me into the kitchen to show me a few things that could be done to a pie to bring out its flavor and enhance its appearance; she called these things "special touches." She said, "It's just another way to express yourself."

Glazed Sugar Top

Before putting the pie in the oven, brush the top with a small amount of milk, then sprinkle with granulated or coarse sugar. Place in the oven and bake according to the recipe.

Flagged Edge

Press together the top and bottom edges of the crust all around the pie, then fold down the edge like a shirt collar. Using kitchen shears or a sharp knife, cut ¼-inch-long slits all the way around about ½ inch apart. Raise up every other tab to a 90-degree angle, so that the design follows a flag up, flag down, flag up, flag down sequence.

Pinched Edge

First, pinch the edge of the crust (or the top and bottom crusts together if it's a double crust pie) all the way around the pie. Next, take a fork and press down into the dough, moving around the entire rim of the pie. Be careful not to press all the way through the dough. For something a little different, crisscross the markings at a 45-degree angle; press the fork down with its tines pointing to the left, then rotate the pie slightly and press down with the tines pointing to the right.

Rope Edge

Place the left index finger and thumb (turned sideways) on your right hand on the border of the pie crust at a 45-degree angle. Gently push your thumb against your index finger to form a slanting ridge all around the pie.

Scalloped Edge

Trim the dough even with the edge of the pie pan. Form a "V" with your right thumb and index finger (about 1 inch apart). Place the "V" on the outside rim of the pie crust. Place the index finger

of your left hand on the inside rim of the crust, inside the "V." Gently pinch your thumb and forefinger, then press down your left forefinger inside the "V" on top of the mound of dough. Don't push all the way through the dough. Follow this push-press, push-press pattern around the rim of the pie. Make sure the scallops are uniform in size.

Lattice Top Mama's Way

When it came to lattice tops, my grandmother had the patience of a snail determined to cross a busy highway. I loved to sit in the kitchen and watch her hand-weave a pie top that looked like

a piece of fine lace when she finished with it. Some women just have a knack for making beautiful things with their hands.

I have always struggled with lattice tops. I just don't have the dexterity it takes to weave the delicate dough in and out, in and out, into a fancy design without the strips tearing or breaking. So when my mother taught me this easy and attractive method, I was elated.

Roll out the dough for a two-crust pie. Place the bottom crust in the pan, leave about ½-inch extension around the rim of the bottom crust. Add the filling. Now, cut the top crust into strips that are about ½ inch wide. Lay half the strips in one direction, going from the top to the bottom of thc pic pan (from 12 o'clock to 6 o'clock). Lay the remaining strips directly on top of those strips going from side to side (from 9 o'clock to 3 o'clock). There is no weaving involved. Trim the ends of the strips evenly with the edge of the dough, then crimp the edges. It bakes up beautifully and no one will care that the strips aren't woven.

Polished Top

Before putting the pie in the oven, brush the top crust with a slightly beaten egg white. If you like, you can also sprinkle a little sugar on top. Place the pie in the oven and bake according to the recipe. The top of the pie will sparkle when you take it out of the oven.

Pie Toppers

Save the trimmings from a double pie crust. Roll them out, then cut out small shapes—diamonds, hearts, stars—with a cookie cutter or a knife. Mix one beaten egg with a teaspoon

of water. Brush the back of each cutout with the egg wash, then lay on the unbaked crust, moistened side down. This won't change the baking time. Sometimes, I'll bake my cutout designs separately on a baking sheet, then arrange them on top of the pie filling after the pie is baked. I might even sprinkle a little colored sugar on top of the cutouts, depending on what I have a taste for.

Sweet Tart Crust

Most tart crusts bake up strong, rich, and crumbly, instead of flaky like pie crusts. Not only does the egg yolk give the dough strength, it also gives it color; the sugar provides sweetness.

This rich pastry can overwhelm a filling, so it's not uncommon to come across a tart recipe that calls for a regular pie crust. Strawberry, lemon, lime, and butterscotch fillings in particular stand up well to this sort of pastry.

9-, 10-, OR 11-INCH SINGLE CRUST

1¼ cups all-purpose flour

¼ cup granulated sugar or firmly packed light brown sugar

½ cup (1 stick) chilled unsalted butter

1 large egg yolk

3 tablespoons ice-cold heavy cream or evaporated milk, more or less as needed

9-, 10-, OR 11-INCH DOUBLE CRUST

2½ cups all-purpose flour

½ cup granulated sugar or firmly packed golden brown sugar

1 cup (2 sticks) chilled unsalted butter

2 large egg yolks

6 tablespoons ice-cold heavy cream or evaporated milk, more or less as needed

Measure the flour and sugar into a medium-size bowl. Using a pastry blender, a big serving fork, or the tips of your fingers, cut in or pinch and squeeze the butter into the dry ingredients until the mixture resembles small garden peas. In a small bowl, whisk the egg yolk until well beaten, then thoroughly work it into the flour mixture with a wooden spoon. When the mixture comes together nicely, shape the dough into a disk, cover with plastic wrap, and refrigerate for at least 1 hour and up to 24 hours before rolling it out.

When you are ready to bake, preheat the oven to 400 degrees. Gather together your pie dish, rolling pin, flour canister, flour sifter, and a small, sharp knife. Prepare a clean surface for rolling out the dough. Sift enough flour over the surface to prevent the dough from sticking to it. Lightly flour your hands and the rolling pin. Place the chilled dough on the surface. (If you are making a double-crust tart, divide the dough into two balls, one slightly larger for the bottom crust. Keep the top crust covered and refrigerated while you roll out the bottom crust.) Press it into a small, flat disk. Roll the dough into a circle, working from the center to the edges. Starting at the center, roll straight up to the edge, turn the dough slightly, and roll straight up to the edge. Repeat the process—turning the dough and rolling—until the dough forms a circle that's slightly larger than the pan. Be careful to keep the dough as even as you can, about ¼ to ⅛ inch thick.

Center the circle of dough over the tart pan, then press it onto the bottom and against the edge of the pan. Firmly roll the rolling pin around the top of the tart pan to trim away the excess dough. To assemble a double crust tart, after fitting the pie pan with the bottom crust and adding the filling, roll out the top crust as large as the pie pan. Fold the dough in half and lay the fold across the center of the pie filling, making sure the edges of the dough reach out and touch the edges of the bottom crust. Unfold the top crust, creating an even, draped effect over the filling as you unfold. Trim the edges, then seal them to the bottom crust by pinching or using the tines of a fork. Cut slits in the top crust to allow the steam to escape.

Prebaking the Crust

For a baked crust that you will be filling later, line the shell with a circle of parchment or waxed paper. Place pie weights or dried beans on top of the paper to prevent the crust from rising out of the pan. Bake until the crust is lightly browned, 10 to 12 minutes, removing the paper and weights a few minutes before the end of the baking time to allow the crust to brown.

2

Berry Pies

Berry season in our small town begins in late June and runs through early September; the strawberries come in around the end of June, the blueberries start to peak around July, and the raspberries come in mid-July and last through the summer. Blackberries arrive in late summer or early fall.

Most women in our town start preparing for berry season way before it hits full swing. All over town you hear women making their berry season declarations: "Summer's comin' and you know what that means—warm weather; time to come out of these concealing sweaters and coats. It's time to head for the gym." Or you'll hear, "I haven't quite made my mind up, but I know I want to do something different with my [hair, makeup, wardrobe, whatever]. I'm sick of the same old look."

In our town, when the weather turns warm and lovely, pretty women blossom on the streets like berries. If you have the eye to see it, you see them as strawberries, blueberries, raspberries, blackberries, even as delectable elderberries. Some are ripe, some are firm, some, you speculate, have ripened too early. But nevertheless, there they are, luscious berries switching up and down the streets in high-heel shoes or whizzing by you, beneath dark sunglasses and convertible car tops. During picking season, most women keep a closer watch on their men; they reconsider before they send them to the streets to do errands that the women could easily do themselves—with all of those juicy berries strutting around out there, I'm sure you understand why.

Unfortunately, if a woman isn't mindful to appreciate herself, to love herself, and embrace her own beauty, berry season can be a terrible time of year; it can have an adverse effect on her self-esteem. A woman will find herself gawking with envy every time a beautiful young woman walks by. She'll let the sights and the fragrant scents of other women keep her trussed in self-doubt, fear, and a perpetual state of jealousy. Berry season can be hard on a woman. I've known women who stay in sullen moods the whole time.

When I was a little girl, most of the members in my family who went to church gathered at my grandmother's house every Sunday morning. (Sometimes there were two carloads of us—Daddy chauffeured one car, my Uncle Ernest, the other.) I didn't understand it then, why my great aunt, Big Mama, upon giving herself one last inspection in the long mirror on my grandmother's chiffonier, would say, "Sister Evans, ya lookin' mighty good this here mornin', even if I have to tell you myself." Now that I'm older, and understand that sometimes the only encouragement a woman gets is the encouragement that she gives herself, I know why it was so necessary for Big Mama to give herself those Sunday morning beauty talks—not just during berry season, but throughout the year as well.

Coral's Blueberry-Peach Cobbler

Coral Raines is the kind of woman other women despise—not because her legs are perfect and her beautiful, cat-colored eyes have a hint of wickedness in them, but because while the rest of us aspiring domestic divas believe there's something trashy about a woman who feeds her man from store-bought mixes, I don't think Coral's ever made anything from scratch. In fact, when we see Coral at the market—switching around the aisles in those black stiletto heels and tight leopard-print dresses that she pours herself into—we can't help but notice that her buggy is overflowing with boxed mixes and prepared dinners that need only water and a microwave to make them table-ready.

What's amazing is that it doesn't bother Coral one bit to strut into one of our community gatherings, toting her semi-homemade cooking and proudly setting it next to entrees that have taken some of us all day to prepare. What's more amazing is that when it's all said and done, despite our best culinary efforts, there's always some good-looking man who'll walk right past our tables of homemade delectables as if they were made of wax, and stroll over to Coral Raines's table, lighting up and carrying on about the wonderful cook that she is. I honestly believe most men take one look at Coral's cat curves and her cat eyes and are convinced that everything about her is *purrrfect*. It reminds me of what my mother used to say: *Infatuation tells us a lot of things that just aren't true.*

If the truth be told, Coral's blueberry-peach cobbler is simple and tasty, even though it is *semi*-homemade. It tastes wonderful topped with a scoop of vanilla ice cream.

- One 10-ounce can sliced peaches in heavy syrup, drained
- ⅛ teaspoon ground nutmeg
- ⅛ teaspoon ground cloves
- 1 teaspoon vanilla extract
- 3 cups blueberry muffin mix
- 1 cup water

Makes one 9 x 13-inch cobbler

Preheat the oven to 350 degrees. Grease a 9 x 13-inch baking dish.

In a large bowl, stir together the peaches, nutmeg, and cloves. Add the vanilla and stir until the peaches are thoroughly coated, then spoon them into the baking dish. In another large bowl, stir together the muffin mix and water until smooth. Spoon the muffin mixture evenly over the peaches. Place in the oven and bake until the top is golden brown, 30 to 35 minutes. Let cool on a wire rack for a few minutes, then serve warm.

Mama's Deep-Dish Strawberry-Rhubarb Pie

My mother loved to bake at night. When I was a little girl, I would sit with her in the kitchen or on the back porch steps while her food was cooking in the oven and she would tell stories.

Mama was a great storyteller. Most of her stories were about other women: happy women, sad women, affluent women, poor women, smart women, and foolish women—black and white. What I remember most about my mother's stories were their punch lines; the little golden nuggets of female truth, summarized in a single sentence or word—all of Mama's stories had them. Some of the punch lines from her stories stand out in my mind more than others, like *Sweet talk can't buy rice* and *What you don't see with your eyes, don't invent with your heart.*

In my family, girly advice gets passed from generation to generation, from woman to woman, just like recipes. Womanish talk is an essential part of becoming a woman. In fact, my mother used to say, "I pity the girl whose mother isn't teaching her anything womanish about life. That kind of girl grows up to be a foolish woman—and we all know that a foolish woman brings out the worst behavior in a man."

Looking back, I don't know what I enjoyed most about our nights together in the kitchen—Mama's stories or the sweet aromas that wafted around our heads. Somehow, once the stories

- ¾ to 1 cup sugar, depending on the sweetness of the fruit, plus more for sprinkling
- ¼ cup all-purpose flour
- ⅛ teaspoon salt
- ⅛ teaspoon ground cinnamon
- ⅛ teaspoon ground cloves
- 3 cups hulled and halved fresh strawberries
- 3 cups 1-inch pieces fresh or (thawed) frozen rhubarb, washed and cut into 1-inch pieces
- 2 tablespoons unsalted butter, cut into small pieces
- Dough for one 9-inch single Flaky Pie Crust (page 8)
- Heavy cream for brushing

Makes one 9-inch pie

and the aromas got to mixing, I was lulled to other times and other places—sometimes to Mama's past, sometimes, to my future.

Mama's deep-dish strawberry-rhubarb pie imparts such a lovely, summer scent that I cook it as much for the fragrance as I do for the taste.

Preheat the oven to 375 degrees.

In a large bowl, combine the sugar, flour, salt, cinnamon, and cloves and mix thoroughly. Add the strawberries and the rhubarb pieces and toss gently until well combined. Let stand for 15 minutes, then toss again and spoon into a 9-inch deep-dish pie plate. Dot the filling with the butter.

On a lightly floured work surface, roll the dough out to a 12-inch square, about ⅛ inch thick. Using a knife or a pastry wheel, cut the dough into ¾- to 1-inch-wide strips. Weave the strips into a lattice pattern on top of the filling. Trim and crimp the ends as you desire. Brush the lattice top with cream; sprinkle lightly with sugar.

Place the pie in the oven and bake until the pastry is golden and the rhubarb tender, 30 to 45 minutes. Let cool completely on a wire rack. To serve, scoop out with a spoon and top each serving with vanilla ice cream or a spoonful of whipped cream.

In my family, girly advice gets passed from generation to generation, from woman to woman, just like recipes.

Marion Newman's Wild Huckleberry Pie

Over the phone, Mama's Cousin Ora tells me that she feels useless. "Day in, day out," she says, "seems like all I'm doin' is sittin' here waitin' to die." When I suggest that she'd feel better about life if she went over to the community center and took a pottery class or signed up for ballroom dance lessons, there is a pause over the line, as if Cousin Ora is bowled over by the absurdity of my proposal. "Child, I'm 76 years old," she says. "I'm too old for such foolishness."

At 76, Miss Marion, my friend's mother, greets you at the door wearing a silk pants suit and elegantly holding a glass of wine, the way they do in the movies. Miss Marion belongs to several social clubs and numerous civic organizations, and is planning a jaunt to Japan. I wonder, at what point does a woman vow to herself that, regardless of age, her life will always be about growth and adventure; that it will encompass more than just sitting around the house, waiting to die?

- 4 cups wild huckleberries or blueberries
- ¾ cup sugar, plus extra for sprinkling
- 3 tablespoons all-purpose flour
- ½ teaspoon ground cinnamon
- Dough for one 9-inch double Flaky Pie Crust (page 8)

Makes one 9-inch pie

Preheat the oven to 400 degrees.

In a large bowl, gently mix together the huckleberries, sugar, flour, and cinnamon.

Gather the dough into two balls, one slightly larger than the other. Refrigerate the smaller one. On a lightly floured surface, roll out the larger ball into a 12-inch circle, ⅛ inch thick. Place a 9-inch pie plate upside down on top of it. Using a small knife, cut around the plate, leaving a 1-inch border of dough around the plate. Remove the plate. Fold one side of the crust over in half, then fold into quarters. Pick up the crust so the center point is positioned in the center of the pie plate. Unfold the dough and press it firmly into the plate. Spoon in the filling. Remove the dough for the top crust from the refrigerator and roll it out to an 11-inch circle in the same way. Lay the top crust over the filling. Trim the overhang to ½ inch. Fold the edge of the top crust under the edge of the bottom crust until they are even with the rim of the plate. Flute all around the edge with your fingers. Sprinkle the top with sugar. Cut slits in the top crust to allow the steam to escape.

Place the pie in the oven and bake until the juices are bubbling up and the top crust is golden brown, about 40 minutes. Miss Marion says she covers the crust edges with a strip of tinfoil so they don't get too brown.

Let cool completely on a wire rack before serving.

Mama's Fresh Raspberry Pie

Long before it was popular, my mother, who never had a career outside of her home, saw herself as much more than *just* a housewife. If the truth be told, she considered herself a kept woman, a domestic geisha, if you will. To keep herself in *that* frame of mind, she wore lovely cotton housedresses and, sometimes, matching marabou slippers while she was doing her housework. And, always, she wore red lipstick.

A large portion of Mama's day was arranged around the time that Daddy was expected to come home from work. His arrival time determined what time she'd start the chicken soaking in the marinade, when she'd go out to the garden and pick the tomatoes for the salad, when she'd set the table. And, when she'd put away her ladies' magazines and run a dust cloth around the living room. Very seldom would Mama allow Daddy to come home from a hard day of working and find her sprawled out, reading magazines and eating homemade chocolates—even if those activities *had* consumed the majority of her day, she didn't want Daddy to know that.

Mama understood that if you are a kept woman, there are certain amenities that the one who is doing the keeping—in Mama's case, Daddy—expects (and deserves) to come home to: a clean house, his woman wearing a crisp housedress (and sometimes, matching marabou slippers), and a well-seasoned meal being a few of them.

Mama was a cunning kept woman. She would time the exact moment that she was pulling her meal out of the oven precisely with Daddy's arrival from work. I will never forget the delighted look on his face when he'd walk through the door, just in time to see Mama taking something delicious out of the oven, especially when she was *staging* one of her fresh raspberry pies. Daddy loved raspberries. Mama used to say, "Men are not as complicated as we make them out to be. The directions below are for a double-crust pie, but you can also prepare these as individual little tartlets with cutouts placed on top, as shown on page 23.

- Dough for one 9-inch double Flaky Pie Crust (page 8)
- 5 cups fresh raspberries, rinsed and drained
- 6 tablespoons all-purpose flour
- ½ cup sugar, or more, depending on the sweetness of the berries
- 1 tablespoon grated lemon rind
- 1 large egg white, lightly beaten
- ⅛ teaspoon ground cinnamon
- 1½ tablespoons unsalted butter
- Milk for brushing (optional)
- Sugar for sprinkling (optional)

Makes one 9-inch pie

Preheat the oven to 425 degrees.

Gather the dough into two balls, one slightly larger than the other. Refrigerate the smaller ball. On a lightly floured work surface, roll out the larger ball of dough into a 12-inch circle about ⅛ inch thick. Place a 9-inch pie plate upside down on top of the rolled-out dough. Using a small knife, cut around the plate, leaving a 1-inch border of dough around the plate. Remove the plate. Fold one side of the crust over in half. Fold the crust into quarters. Pick up the crust so that the center point is positioned in the center of the plate. Unfold the dough and press it firmly into the pie plate.

In a large bowl, combine the raspberries, flour, sugar, and lemon rind and gently toss to combine, then set the bowl aside.

Using a pastry brush, brush the inside of the bottom crust with the egg whites, then spoon in the filling. Sprinkle the top of the filling with cinnamon, then dot it with the butter.

Remove the dough for the top crust from the refrigerator and roll it out into an 11-inch circle the same way you rolled out the bottom crust. Lay the top crust over the filling. To dress up the pie, press together the top and bottom edges of the crust all around the pie, then fold down the edge like a shirt collar. Using kitchen shears or a sharp knife, cut ¼-inch-long slits all the way around, about ½-inch apart. Raise up every other tab to a 90-degree angle, so there's a flag up, flag down, flag up, flag down design running around the rim. Cut slits in the crust to allow the steam to escape. If you like, you can brush the top with milk and sprinkle with a scant amount of sugar.

Place the pie in the oven on a cookie sheet. Bake for 15 minutes, then reduce the oven temperature to 350 degrees and bake until the crust is golden, another 35 to 40 minutes. Cover the edge of the crust with a 2- to 3-inch-wide strip of aluminum foil if it starts to brown excessively. Let cool to room temperature on a wire rack.

Joyce Carol's Black and Blue Pie

My mother's friend Joyce Carol says she entered this recipe in a community contest over 35 years ago; she says it was a runner up. However, she swears it would have taken first place if Old Lady Hattie Tinsley hadn't been the only culinary judge that year. According to Joyce Carol, Old Lady Tinsley's favorite niece, Irene, was also a cooking contestant that year. According to Joyce Carol, Irene took first place in every one of the food categories.

They say everybody in town knew the truth of the matter, that Irene was a pitiful cook. But in a small town, when you've got an auntie like Hattie Tinsley, who donates to the charities and sits on all of the boards and knows everybody worth knowing, it would be hard not to take advantage of it.

In my mind, there's no doubt about it, if it hadn't been for Old Lady Hattie Tinsley's meddling, Joyce Carol's black and blue pie would have taken home a first place ribbon.

- Dough for one 9-inch double Flaky Pie Crust (page 8)
- ¾ cup sugar
- ⅓ cup all-purpose flour
- ¼ teaspoon ground cloves
- ⅛ teaspoon ground nutmeg
- 4 cups fresh blueberries, picked over
- 1½ cups fresh blackberries, picked over
- ½ teaspoon vanilla extract
- 1 tablespoon fresh lemon juice
- 2 tablespoons unsalted butter, cut into small pieces

Makes one 9-inch pie

Preheat the oven to 450 degrees

Gather the dough into two balls, one slightly larger than the other. Refrigerate the smaller one. On a lightly floured work surface, roll out the larger one into a 12-inch circle, about ⅛ inch thick. Place a 9-inch pie plate upside down on top of it. Using a small knife, cut around the plate, leaving a 1-inch border of dough around the plate. Remove the plate. Fold one side of the crust over in half, fold it the crust into quarters. Pick up so that the center point is positioned in the center of the pie plate. Unfold the dough and press it firmly into the plate.

In a large bowl, combine the sugar, flour, cloves, and nutmeg. Gently stir in the berries and vanilla until well coated, then pour into the bottom crust. Sprinkle with the lemon juice and dot with the butter.

Remove the dough for the top crust from the refrigerator and roll out to an 11-inch circle in the same way. Lay the top crust over the filling. Seal the top and bottom crusts, then crimp the edges. Cut steam vents in the top with a knife. Cover the edge of the pie with 2- to 3-inch-wide strips of aluminum foil. Place in the oven and bake until the top turns golden, 35 to 45 minutes. (I always remove the foil the last 10 minutes of baking.) Let cool to room temperature on a wire rack before serving.

Dezarae Triplett's Mixed Berry Pie

Dezarae Triplett was one of those lovely young housewives in the neighborhood whom little girls emulate when they play house and dress-up. I adored Miss Dezarae. She wore mink coats and diamond earrings and her young husband, Sterling, was the best looking husband that I had ever seen.

Not only was Miss Dezarae pretty—long, wavy hair and smooth, glowing skin the color of fresh honey—she was also as sweet as strawberries and extremely artsy with her kitchen adornments and the ornate little trinkets she placed throughout her vegetable garden out back. When Miss Dezarae and her live-in mother-in-law, Miss Alma, invited us to stop by to pick mustards, turnips, collards, and kale, my mother and I were elated. Miss Dezarae was one of those women who always had something sweet and cold from her refrigerator and something freshly baked from her oven to offer when she invited you inside. We especially liked to stop by during berry season. Miss Dezarae always had a berry pie sitting on the counter—and it was always close to perfect.

Of course, I used to hear Mama say, "Ain't nothin' perfect. If you look at anything close enough, you can find a little something wrong with it."

Take Miss Dezarae's seemingly ideal life, for instance. They say her pretty husband, Sterling, was too much of a mama's boy. They say his mama, Miss Alma, was always whining about

Dough for one 9-inch double Flaky Pie Crust (page 8)
1 cup sugar
⅛ teaspoon salt
3 tablespoons all-purpose flour
½ teaspoon ground cinnamon
1 cup fresh blueberries, picked over
1 cup hulled and sliced fresh strawberries
¾ cup fresh blackberries, picked over
¾ cup fresh red raspberries, picked over
½ cup water
1 tablespoon fresh lemon juice
2 tablespoons unsalted butter, cut into small pieces
Milk for brushing
Coarse sugar for sprinkling

Makes one 9-inch pie

something, always trying to set Sterling and Dezarae against one another—that she gave poor Dezarae the blues. They say, when you saw Sterling and Dezarae *and* Miss Alma out on their Sunday drives—Miss Alma riding shotgun—it was because the young couple had no other choice. Say they couldn't go anywhere without Miss Alma; how could they? Say she owned the family car *and* the house they lived in. Some claimed she owned the mink coats and the diamond earrings that Miss Dezarae wore so well.

They tell me, the kitchen was the only place where Miss Alma didn't have power over Miss Dezarae. Say, for a country woman, Miss Alma couldn't cook a decent meal to save her meddling life—say she couldn't boil water without burning it. My mother, who had a penchant for sticking up for the mistreated, could be a real smart aleck when she wanted to. Mama loved to put Miss Alma in her place. Mama would say, "This is the most delicious berry pie that I've ever put in my mouth; who made it?" knowing full well how much it aggravated Miss Alma to admit that her daughter-in-law could outdo her in the kitchen. Of course, Miss Alma whose word was usually law, would retort with something like, "Dezarae left it in the oven too long, it's too crispy 'round the edges," or "It's a trifle too sweet for my taste," to which Mama would insist, "Now, Miss Alma, a person would have to be lookin' through a magnifying glass to find something wrong with this pie; like I said, it's the best berry pie I've ever tasted." Mama said Miss Alma would look indignant; said her nose would be turned up like a stiff shirt collar. Say, she'd walk out of the room just as nice and quiet as you please; say you wouldn't hear another peep out of her.

Preheat the oven to 400 degrees.

Gather the dough into two balls, one slightly larger than the other. Refrigerate the smaller ball of dough. On a lightly floured work surface, roll out the larger ball of dough into a 12-inch circle, about ⅛ inch thick. Place a 9-inch pie plate upside down on top of the rolled-out dough. Using a small knife, cut around the plate, leaving a 1-inch border of dough around the plate. Remove the plate. Fold one side of the crust over in half. Fold the crust into quarters. Pick up the crust so that the center point is positioned in the center of the plate. Unfold the dough and press it firmly into the pie plate. Refrigerate the bottom crust.

Combine the sugar, salt, flour, and cinnamon in a large saucepan. Add the berries and gently toss with the sugar mixture until coated. Add the water and lemon juice and cook over medium heat just to the boiling point, stirring often. Remove the bottom crust and the smaller ball of dough from the refrigerator. Pour the filling into the pie crust and dot with the butter. On a lightly floured surface, roll it out to an 11-inch circle, about 1/8 inch thick and either place on top of the filling or cut it into 3/4-inch-wide lattice strips an weave them on top of the filling. Be sure to cut slits in the top to release the steam if you opt for a full crust. Brush with milk and sprinkle with a little coarse sugar.

Reduce the oven temperature to 350 degrees and bake until the berries bubble and the crust is golden brown, about 45 minutes. Let cool completely on a wire rack before serving.

They tell me, the kitchen was the only place Miss Alma didn't have power over Miss Dezarae.

Strawberry Hand Pies for the Welcoming Table

FILLING

3½ cups fresh strawberries, hulled and sliced

1¼ cups sugar

3 tablespoons cornstarch

1 teaspoon fresh lemon juice

FRIED PIE DOUGH

1½ cups plus 2 tablespoons all-purpose flour

½ teaspoon salt

½ cup chilled vegetable shortening

3 to 5 tablespoons ice water, more or less as needed

1 small egg beaten together with 2 tablespoons heavy cream or milk

⅓ cup vegetable shortening, for frying

Makes 8 pies

My Aunt Marjell is a wonderful person to visit. Unlike a lot of the people you visit these days, people who open their front doors and immediately start peeping around to see what gifts and trinkets you might have brought them (to show how grateful you are for having been invited to their houses, I guess), Aunt Marjell has always been just the opposite. She goes out of her way to delight and pamper her guests, to make her company feel appreciated. When you're on your way to Aunt Marjell's house, you get tickled 'cause you know she's gonna have a little treat waiting on you—her gracious manner and a little something sweet that says, "Thank you for stopping by."

Aunt Marjell, who once told me that it's a sin to mistreat a guest in your home, says, "The same rules of hospitality apply to the man you're with. Sometimes a man can make you feel like using cuss words that would disgrace a bartender in a beer hall, but remember, while on the inside you're screaming, 'Shoo cat! Shoo!' there may be another woman on the outside purring, 'Here, kitty, kitty, here.'"

It doesn't matter if she's handing them out when I get there or if she's passing them out just before I leave, when I see a platter of Aunt Marjell's strawberry hand pies, it makes me happy that I stopped by.

Make the filling. Gently toss the strawberries and sugar together in a large bowl, cover with plastic wrap, and refrigerate overnight. In the morning, remove from the refrigerator. Combine the cornstarch and lemon juice in a large saucepan and stir until there are no lumps. Add the strawberries, along with the juice that's formed. Bring the mixture to a boil over medium heat. Reduce the heat to low and continue to cook until the mixture thickens, about 3 minutes, stirring often. Remove from the heat and let cool completely.

Prepare the fried pie dough. Combine the flour and salt in a large bowl. Work the chilled shortening in with your fingers, pinching it into the flour mixture until it resembles tiny split peas. Add the water, 1 tablespoon at a time, until the dough is moist and comes together to form a smooth disk. Do not overmix. Form the dough into a disk, wrap tightly in plastic wrap, and refrigerate for at least 30 minutes.

To form the pies, remove the dough from the refrigerator and let stand for 6 to 7 minutes. Lightly flour your rolling pin and work surface, divide the dough into 8 equal portions, and roll each portion out to ⅛-inch thickness. Brush each circle with the egg wash. Place about 3 tablespoons of the cooled strawberry mixture on one-half of each circle. Leave about 1 inch of dough around the outer edge. Fold the other half of the circle over the strawberry filling, all the way to the edge. Crimp the edges together with the tines of a fork, sealing the pie completely.

In a large, heavy frying pan, heat about 1 inch of vegetable shortening. Fry a few of the hand pies at a time until golden brown, 3 to 5 minutes per side. Add more shortening if needed. Remove the pies with a slotted metal spoon and drain on paper towels before serving.

These taste good with a sprinkle of confectioner's sugar.

When you're on your way to Aunt Marjell's house, you get tickled 'cause you know she's gonna have a little treat waiting on you—her gracious manner and a little something sweet that says, "Thank you for stopping by."

Miss Viola Tresvant's Blueberry Pie with the Crumb Topping

Shortly after Miss Viola Tresvant, a normally good-natured woman from the old neighborhood, started going through her *change of life*, they say poor Miss Viola suffered one crying spell right after the other. They say if her husband Morgan, so much as brushed by without smiling or telling her how much he adored her, she was prone to burst into a fit of tears that could last—give or take a few hours—the rest of the day.

Well, as every woman knows, if you cry too often, your tears will eventually lose their effect. Such was eventually the case with Miss Viola and her husband. Where he used to rush to comfort his wife at the first sign of a sniffle, it got to the place where Miss Viola could cry a river and the only attention that Morgan gave the matter was when he'd peek at her from the top of his newspaper, shake his head, then resume reading seemingly unmoved by the sight of what he had started referring to as *one of Viola's hissy fits*.

My mother used to say, *When you lose your influence with a man, you've lost your power.*

When she saw that her tears were no longer moving *her*
him with her cooking—

Miss Viola might have been going through her change and therefore experiencing bouts of wild crying, but she wasn't about to let Morgan disregard her at a time in her life when she needed him to be his most compassionate. After all, she had coddled him through many of *his* little episodes. She'd baby-talked him back to his senses when his "bright idea" to quit his good-paying General Motors job (in order to start up a neighborhood bowling alley) would have set them back for years had he gone through with it. She'd followed him from place to place in a rickety, rented, secondhand RV during his wanderlust period. And when the bald spot at the back of his head spread to the size of a Mason jar lid and sent him on a tail-chase concerning his thinning good looks, she was steadfast in doling out a daily dose of compliments designed to make him feel like a new man. When she saw that her tears were no longer *moving* her husband, they tell me Miss Viola decided to *touch* him with her cooking—Morgan loved to eat.

When Miss Viola's change-of-life moods overtook her, especially when she felt forsaken by her husband, she'd set a sparse dinner table—nothing more distinguished than a bowl of unseasoned meat broth and a chunk of day-old, hot-water bread. But when she felt good, when she felt loved and appreciated, she'd go all out—fried chicken, smothered white potatoes, mustard greens and smoked ham hocks, skillet cornbread, sun tea. And Miss Viola's blueberry pie with the crumb topping that Morgan loved so much.

They say, shortly after Miss Viola started cooking according to how she felt, Morgan began paying more attention to his wife; they say, sweet-talking his wife and keeping her in a good mood became his area of expertise.

husband, they tell me that Miss Viola decided to touch
Morgan loved to eat.

Preheat the oven to 400 degrees. Prepare the pie crust and set aside.

Make the crumb topping. In a medium-size bowl, stir together the flour, brown sugar, and cinnamon until well mixed. Work the butter in with a fork or your fingertips until the mixture resembles crumbs the size of tiny sweet-peas. Set aside.

Make the filling. In a large bowl, stir together the sugar and flour until well mixed. Gently stir in the blueberries and lemon rind and juice. Pour the mixture into the pie crust, then dot it with the pieces of butter. Sprinkle the crumb topping evenly over the top of the pie.

Reduce the oven temperature to 350 degrees. Place the pie in the oven and bake until the topping is golden brown, 40 to 45 minutes. Let cool completely on a wire rack before serving. This looks and tastes wonderful with a dollop of vanilla ice cream sitting on top.

One 9-inch single Flaky Pie crust (page 8), rolled out, fitted into a pie plate, and edge trimmed and crimped

CRUMB TOPPING

1 cup all-purpose flour

½ cup firmly packed brown sugar

½ teaspoon ground cinnamon

½ cup (1 stick) chilled unsalted butter, cut into pieces

FILLING

½ cup granulated sugar

¼ cup all-purpose flour

4 cups fresh blueberries, picked over

½ teaspoon finely grated lemon rind

1 tablespoon fresh lemon juice

2 tablespoons unsalted butter, cut into pieces

Makes one 9-inch pie

Victoria's Secrets (and Her Berry Patch Cobbler)

I have plenty of work clothes and church clothes and *womanish* clothes to wear to the front door to let my boyfriend in, but I've always had trouble putting together a wardrobe for the *cocktail hour*. I just can't seem to find the right dressy-dressy stuff for my body, my budget, and my social-life requirements. By the time I add something "after five" to my wardrobe, somebody on the television is proclaiming it out of season. So I finally gave up. I went out and bought myself a couple of basic blacks—skirts and little dresses—and just stopped trying to be glitzy.

But every now and then, I'll get a call from one of my fashionable friends, and she'll have tickets to this or to that, and something will come over me and I just can't help myself; I'm just not gonna let the other woman outdo me this time. So I immediately get on the phone with Vicky Cook, my friend since kindergarten. I'll say something like, "Girl, I need something pretty to wear to such and such," and Vicky will say, "You know you're more than welcome to come over and go through my closet."

Going through Vicky's closet is like a kid going through the proverbial candy store. In fact, Vicky's closet is full of dresses and hats and shoes and purses in all kinds of candy-like colors. And then there's the black-tie stuff: dark, rich colors with ruffles, beading, and attached brooches, minks, leathers, chiffons, feathers, and a velvet jewelry box holding her faux jewels and another one for the real stuff. When you walk inside Vicky's closet, your mouth drops to the floor. When she pulls out a drawer from her dresser, the neatly folded garments give off an amazingly soft and spicy aroma that permeates the room. It's like being in Girlie Paradise.

I keep telling myself that one of these days I'm going to have my own little *womanly* renaissance; I'm gonna go through my lingerie drawers and neatly arrange my bras and panties and nighties the way Mama used to tell me a woman's intimate drawers should be arranged. I'm gonna hang my stuff on satin hangers and hide fragrant sachets inside my dresser. I'm going to take a few days off and go to Saks and Lord & Taylor and Nordstroms, and . . . the

Salvation Army (hey, they tell me you can find some nice stuff at the secondhand stores). At each store, I'm going to take my time and stand in front of a mirror until I get my *cocktail hour* wardrobe right. And then, when one of my girlfriends calls me complaining that she doesn't have anything fancy to wear to this or to that, I'm gonna stick my chest out proudly and say nonchalantly what Vicky always says, "You know, you're more than welcome to come by and go through my closet."

Victoria's secrets aren't limited to putting together a fantastic wardrobe. She's also a marvelous cook and she's shared more than a few of her baking secrets with me, like: A good berry pie must begin with plump, ripe berries; and if you're using a glass dish, check the bottom crust. Let the pie cook until the crust is golden brown, much like the color of a paper bag. The more color in the crust, the tastier it'll be. And whatever you do, don't worry if your pie isn't picture perfect—when you put your own stamp on it, that's what gives scratch cooking its advantage over store-bought.

- 1 cup plus 1 tablespoon sugar
- 3 tablespoons quick-cooking tapioca
- 2 cups fresh blueberries, picked over
- 2 cups hulled and halved fresh strawberries
- 1 cup fresh blackberries, picked over
- 1 cup fresh raspberries, picked over
- Dough for one 9-inch double Flaky Pie Crust (page 8)
- 2 tablespoons unsalted butter, cut into small pieces

Makes one 9-inch pie

Preheat the oven to 375 degrees.

In a large bowl, stir together 1 cup of the sugar and the tapioca. Add the berries and gently toss until well coated with sugar. Set aside.

Divide the pie dough in half. On a lightly floured work surface, roll out one half into a 12-inch circle, about ⅛ inch thick. Fit it into a 9-inch pie plate. Trim the pastry to ½ inch beyond the rim of the plate. Pour the berry mixture into the crust. Dot the filling with the butter. Roll out the remaining pie dough into a square about ⅛ inch thick. Cut the pastry into ¾-inch-wide strips. Sprinkle the remaining 1 tablespoon sugar evenly over the strips. Weave the strips into a lattice pattern over the top of the filling. Press the ends of the strips into the edge of the bottom crust. Fold the bottom pastry upward, over the strip ends. Press around the edge of the pie with the tines of a large fork. To prevent overbrowning, cover the edge of the pie with aluminum foil.

Place the pie in the oven and bake until the top is nicely golden, about 30 minutes. Let cool completely on a wire rack before serving with a scoop of vanilla ice cream.

Old-Fashioned Cranberry Pie

When I was a little girl, Luther and Elizabeth King were an older couple who lived in a big, white house that was so immaculate you could eat off the sidewalk in front of their house and not get a speck of dirt on your tongue. Luther was so particular, in late fall, he would stand on a wooden ladder, donning his scout-master's safari hat and bleached white gardening gloves, and hand-pick the leaves off the trees in his yard so they wouldn't fall on top of his perfect lawn.

When my parents moved away from the old neighborhood, they remained friends with Luther and Elizabeth. Some Saturdays, Miss Elizabeth would call Mama and say, "Come to dinner tomorrow; we'll have turkey and dressing and cranberry pie, and afterward we'll go into the living room and watch the *Ed Sullivan Show*." Miss Elizabeth was an excellent cook and Luther owned a floor-model color TV; my young parents didn't need a whole lot of persuasion to accept Miss Elizabeth's invitation. Mama loved good cooking and recipe swapping and Daddy loved state-of-the-art electronics. I loved cuddling up with Princess, Miss Elizabeth's old and nervous chihuahua. It would have been a perfect Sunday outing except for the fact that Luther, who was so sweet and mannerly toward everybody else in the house, treated Miss Elizabeth like a dragonfly that had slipped in through an open window.

As soon as we stepped inside their house, like Edith Bunker, Miss Elizabeth came trotting to the door to retrieve our wraps, and she never stopped trotting the whole time we were there. One minute she was bringing us a glass of something cold, the next, fluffing our pillows, or lifting our feet onto cushiony ottomans. She would ask us, over and over, "Can I get you anything? Is everything alright?" Miss Elizabeth was constantly on her feet, constantly scurrying between me and my parents, Luther and the kitchen, because, like Archie Bunker, Luther barked out orders the whole time we were there. He would say things like, "Lizabeth! Answer the phone. *Lizabeth, Lizabeth, Lizabeth!*"—it went on and on with Luther.

My mother used to say, *An unhappy husband will ask you for toasted snow.*

Once, as Miss Elizabeth was pushing back from the dinning room table—she was on her way to fetch the butter dish that she had left on the kitchen counter—Luther shook his head and said,

"Woman's a scatterbrain; most of the time she forgets to use the sense she was born with."

On the way home, Mama started crying. When Daddy asked her what was wrong, Mama sobbed, "I just can't stand to see him treat her that way. I never want to go there again." The next day, Daddy went out and bought us our first floor-model color TV. As a family, we never went back to Luther and Miss Elizabeth's house.

Years later, Mama confided in me that she had willed herself to cry that day. Said she didn't want to go back to Luther's house with Daddy because she didn't want Daddy, a young man who was still learning how to be a husband, to look at Luther and get the wrong idea.

Mama continued to exchange recipes over the phone with Miss Elizabeth. They remained phone-friends until Miss Elizabeth passed away in the late seventies.

Miss Elizabeth's cranberry pie is a lovely one that goes well with a turkey-and-dressing Sunday dinner. Now, whenever I make it, I think about Miss Elizabeth—she was such a kindhearted woman. I pray that wherever she is, she's somewhere with Princess curled on her lap, and her feet resting on a cushiony ottoman. Lord knows, Miss Elizabeth has done her share of trotting.

- Dough for one 9-inch double Flaky Pie Crust (page 8)
- 2 cups fresh cranberries, picked over
- 1½ cups dark raisins
- ½ cup chopped walnuts
- ¼ cup granulated sugar
- ⅓ cup firmly packed dark brown sugar
- ½ teaspoon vanilla extract
- ½ teaspoon orange extract
- Grated rind of 1 medium-size orange
- ⅛ teaspoon salt
- 2 tablespoons unsalted butter, cut into small pieces

Makes one 9-inch pie

Line a cookie sheet with waxed paper and set aside. Preheat the oven to 425 degrees.

Gather the dough into two balls, one slightly larger than the other. On a lightly floured work surface, roll out the larger ball into an 11-inch circle, about ⅛ inch thick. Press the crust into a 9-inch pie plate. Now, roll out the top crust the same way as you did the bottom crust. Using a knife, cut the dough into lattice strips ½ inch wide. Arrange the strips on the prepared cookie sheet. Refrigerate the bottom crust and lattice strips until they are needed.

In a large bowl, combine the cranberries, raisins, walnuts, and both sugars and toss until mixed well. Stir in the extracts, orange rind, and salt.

Remove the crust from the refrigerator and pour the filling into it. Dot with the butter. Remove the lattice strips from the refrigerator. Weave a lattice design over the top of the pie. Trim and crimp the edges together. Bake for 12 minutes, then reduce the oven temperature to 350 degrees. Continue to bake until the crust is golden, 35 to 45 minutes. Let cool completely before serving.

3

Cereal Pies

One prevailing myth in our culture is, what you see is what you get. To that end, most of us—if the truth be told—have an aversion to the unadorned. For example, my grandmother wouldn't serve her desserts on anything but her good china because she believed her sweets tasted better when they were plated on something pretty. And my mother's cousin Addie, who wears tons of flashy charms around her neck and on her fingers and arms (and clipped to her ears), considers herself to be the finest thing walking, due to all of that adornment. But over the years I've learned that sometimes the simple in life can really fool you; it can sneak up on you and be so full of richness and flavor—this applies to people as well as pies—that, once you get a taste of it, it nearly takes your breath away. Our culture ought to learn to be more tolerant of the unadorned; it ought to give the plain in life at least a chance before it rushes on over to the adorned.

This reminds me of what my mother used to say, "You may want a handsome husband, but do you really need one?" The same goes for pies. A pie doesn't have to call for elaborate ingredients to taste delicious.

Oatmeal Nut Pie

- One 9-inch single Flaky Pie Crust (page 8), rolled out, fitted into a pie plate, and edge trimmed and crimped
- 4 large eggs, well beaten
- ½ cup granulated sugar
- ½ cup firmly packed light brown sugar
- ¼ cup (½ stick) unsalted butter, melted and cooled
- 1 cup milk
- 2 tablespoons all-purpose flour
- 1 teaspoon vanilla extract
- ½ teaspoon maple-flavored extract
- ¼ cup dark corn syrup
- ¼ cup quick-cooking oats
- ½ cup chopped pecans
- ½ cup sweetened shredded coconut

Makes one 9-inch pie

This recipe came to me from my sweet cousin Stephanie, whom everybody calls "the peacemaker" between us girl cousins, because whenever one of us is puffed up about something, Stephanie is the first one to go out of her way to bring the obstinate one back into the fold. But when it comes to recipes, don't let Stephanie's tenderhearted nature fool you. She guards her wonderful recipes like a movie star guards her jewels; you have to catch her in the right mood to get one out of her. However, please don't hold that against Steph, it's just the way we were raised. My grandmother once said, "There's something immoral about a woman who'll give out her recipes to anyone who asks."

I have to tell you, this is one of my favorite pies. And I believe it will become one of your favorites, too. It tastes like a slice of paradise to the taste buds.

Preheat the oven to 350 degrees. Prepare the crust and set aside.

In a large bowl, combine the eggs, both sugars, butter, and milk until well mixed. Stir in the flour, extracts, and corn syrup until well mixed. Blend in the oats, pecans, and coconut. Pour the filling into the pie crust.

To give it a nice little edge, place your left index finger and your right thumb (turned sideways) on the border of the pie crust at a 45-degree angle. Gently push your thumb against your index finger to form a pretty slanting ridge all around the pie. Place in the oven and bake until the filling is nice and golden, 45 to 50 minutes. Let cool on a wire rack.

You may serve this delectable pie warm or at room temperature—I prefer the latter.

Cousin Gracie's Grape-Nuts® Pie

Whoever said, no two people have the same reality, must have been talking about my grandmother's third cousins, Gracie and Grace's sister Gladys—we called them Cousin Gracie and Cousin Gladie. While Cousin Gracie was always praising the Lord and giving thanks for the little that she had, every time we saw Cousin Gladie, she was frowning and expressing her sorrow for not having more. While Cousin Gracie saw the glass as half full, Cousin Gladie saw the glass as a reminder that she didn't have the money to go to town and buy herself a new set.

You may not believe it, but it's true: Cousin Gracie's gratitude made a huge difference in her cooking. While Cousin Gracie could take a sack and make it taste good, Cousin Gladie had trouble boiling water.

Cousin Gracie's Grape-Nuts pie is tasty and easy to make. It reminds me of her agreeable demeanor. Whenever I take it somewhere, the people just love it.

- One 9-inch single Flaky Pie Crust (page 8), rolled out, fitted into a pie plate, and edge trimmed and crimped
- ½ cup Grape-Nuts cereal
- ½ cup warm water
- 3 large eggs, well beaten
- ¾ cup sugar
- 1 cup dark corn syrup
- ⅛ teaspoon salt
- 1 teaspoon vanilla extract
- ¼ cup (½ stick) unsalted butter, melted

Makes one 9-inch pie

Preheat the oven to 350 degrees. Prepare the pie crust and set aside.

Combine the Grape-Nuts and warm water in a medium-size bowl. Let stand until the water is absorbed into the cereal. In a large bowl, combine the eggs, sugar, corn syrup, salt, vanilla, and melted butter and stir until mixed well. Fold in the Grape-Nuts, then spoon the filling into the crust. Place in the oven and bake until a toothpick inserted off center comes out clean, about 50 minutes. Let cool completely on a wire rack before serving.

Old-Fashioned Cornflake Pie

Sometimes Mama would shake her head when she got off the phone after a long conversation with one of her girlfriends. She would say, "Thank God, for Ruthie (or Catherine or Thelma or Mabeline). I sure do appreciate her encouragement." Mama always paid verbal homage to her girlfriends. She would tell me things like, "Can't nobody fry chicken like Thelma . . . . It's because of Ruthie that I love to read . . . . Catherine is the most loyal friend . . . . That Mabeline is a mess." Mama despised the kind of men who tried to come between their women and their women's true friends. She used to tell me, "You don't want a man who's jealous of nothin' *or* everything."

My mother believed that every woman should have an older woman friend to lean on when she's going through tough times, and a younger woman friend to keep her from growing old too soon. Dee, whom I've been friends with for years, is my younger friend and she encourages me to see things outside of their proverbial boxes. She is just as likely to stop by with a controversial new book in hand as she is to come bearing a form-fitting mini dress that she'll thrust in my arms. "Let's go out on the town tonight; and I don't wanna hear nothing 'bout, *I don't have anything to wear* 'cause I brought you something."

It doesn't surprise me at all that Dedrea would look "outside of the box" and come up with such a fun and delicious use for something that most people can't see using past breakfast.

One 9-inch single deep-dish Flaky Pie Crust (page 8), rolled out, fitted into the pie plate, and edge trimmed and crimped

⅔ cup sugar

⅔ cup dark corn syrup

3 large eggs

1 teaspoon vanilla extract

3 tablespoons unsalted butter, melted

⅛ teaspoon salt

2 cups coarsely crushed cornflakes (I put the flakes in a medium-size bowl and give them a couple of quick punches with my fist)

Makes one 9-inch deep-dish pie

Preheat the oven to 350 degrees. Prepare the pie crust and set aside.

Thoroughly mix together the sugar and corn syrup in a large bowl. Crack the eggs, one at a time, over a small bowl. Beat them well, then stir them into the sugar mixture. Add the vanilla, melted butter, and salt and stir until blended. Fold in the crushed cornflakes until well coated. Pour the filling into the pie crust, place in the oven, and bake until a knife inserted in the center comes out clean, 45 to 50 minutes. Let cool completely on a wire rack. A scoop of vanilla ice cream does this pie good.

The Missus and Her Granola Pie

Nineteen was a pivotal age for my mother. She was nineteen when she moved to Michigan, nineteen when she opened up her first charge account, and nineteen when she bought her first piece of furniture—an ornate chiffonier that I still have today. Mama was nineteen when she got her first job in Michigan working as a weekday, live-in nanny for the two children of a family that owned a large car dealership. In fact, the wealthy family had two live-ins: Mama and an older, spinsterish German woman named Gretchen. Gretchen did most of the cooking for the family, while Mama mostly managed their two children; she brushed their hair, read to them, took them for walks around their high-class neighborhood, and put them down for their naps. The parents believed in order and discipline, they didn't pamper their children unnecessarily the way some wealthy people did. They even allowed Mama to use a mild amount of corporal punishment—the back side of a hairbrush—when the children were acting out.

Mama often talked about the family, about the wonderful way they treated her, especially *The Missus*; that's what Mama and Gretchen called the lady of the house. According to Mama, The Missus was an attractive woman with modern values and ash-blond hair. She was a confident, well-polished kind of woman, who appeared unmoved by the fact that her husband often carpooled to work with his shapely secretary Brenda. Mama said the girl would pull up some mornings, toot the horn on her convertible Cadillac, and *The Mister* would go rushing

The Missus was an attractive woman with modern values and ash-blond hair. She was a confident, well-polished kind of woman.

out the door, the way a dog rushes out to his master. Mama used to say, "Even though I was a young, inexperienced girl at the time, as far as I was concerned, The Mister seemed a little too happy to go to work on the mornings that Brenda drove him in." But it didn't seem to faze The Missus. According to Mama, The Missus never *ever* spoke hateful about Brenda or The Mister.

In the summertime, The Missus often went on a solo weekend holiday in the woods of Upper Michigan. According to Mama, the family had a beautiful cabin on the lake. Many times, The Missus would ask Mama to accompany her. She'd assure Mama that she was asking more for Mama's company than for the occasional sandwich or pitcher of lemonade she would ask my mother to serve.

For the most part, my mother loved going up North with The Missus. The Missus drove a light-colored, convertible Cadillac similar to Brenda's. Mama liked the woodsy scenery and the fact that there wasn't much to do during the day. The Missus went from one party in the woods to the next. Mama had the beautiful, well-stocked cabin to herself; in fact, she used to say, "It was as much a holiday for me, as it was for The Missus."

At some point, though, the holiday in the woods almost always ended with some strange man—at least strange to Mama—delivering home a drunken Missus. Sometimes there were two strange men—one at each end—carrying The Missus through the woods as if she were a sack of flour. Mama said, The Missus's hair would be disheveled, the buttons on her blouse wouldn't be lined up correctly, and her lipstick would be smeared onto her cheeks like an abstract painting. Mama said most of the men were mannerly, regardless of what they had or had not done to The Missus on their way to bringing her home. Mama said the men would put

The Missus to bed, then promptly leave, except for maybe one or two who paused long enough to eyeball Mama. Mama was an attractive, intelligent girl, with an old-fashioned, pearls-and-red-lipstick demeanor that appealed to most men—black and white—in those days.

Gretchen, the German housekeeper-cook, who often said that my mother was the kind of girl she would have been proud to have given birth to, would always ask Mama about the weekends in the woods. She was particularly curious as to why The Missus always made something sweet and special, like this granola pie, for Mama as soon as they returned. Gretchen thought it looked a lot like a bribe—but Mama never told Gretchen (or The Mister) about the things that went on in the woods up North. The only person she ever told the *whole* story to was me, when she would call me to the kitchen to talk about womanish things, and how nineteen had been a pivotal age in her life.

- One 9-inch single Flaky Pie Crust (page 8), rolled out, fitted in a pie plate, and edge trimmed and crimped
- 1 cup light corn syrup
- ¾ cup firmly packed dark brown sugar
- 3 large eggs, slightly beaten
- ¼ cup (½ stick) unsalted butter, melted
- 1 teaspoon vanilla extract
- ⅛ teaspoon salt
- 1 heaping cup coarsely crushed granola cereal, without raisins

Makes one 9-inch pie

Preheat the oven to 375 degrees. Prepare the pie crust and set aside.

In a large bowl, combine the corn syrup, brown sugar, eggs, butter, vanilla, and salt until well blended. Stir in the cereal until fully blended. Pour the filling into the pie crust. Place in the oven and bake until the filling is set and the crust nice and golden, 40 to 50 minutes. (During the last 15 to 20 minutes of baking, you can apply a band of aluminum foil around the edge of the crust to prevent it from overbrowning.) Let cool completely on a wire rack before serving. You can top this pie with whipped cream or vanilla ice cream if you want to, but it tastes just as good plain.

Caramel Tin Roof Pie

Daddy grew up in a Tennessee farmhouse that sat on 88 acres of land. From what they tell me, Grandmother was a country cook, capable of winning ribbons. They say, she made the best cobblers and her homemade ice cream was divine. Daddy was used to eating well and he really loved ice cream.

Mama was the kind of woman Daddy needed. She practically lived at the grocery store; she was always there, looking for new ways to spruce up Daddy's suppers. When I was growing up, there was always a gallon of vanilla ice cream in our deep freezer. Seems to me, we had a serving of it every other night, under various sauces, scooped on top of a slice of pie, or stuffed inside of a fresh waffle cone, but we liked it best when Mama used it to crown a slice of her tin roof pie.

My mother started making this pie in the late 1960s/early 1970s. It was part of her repertoire of trendy entrees—sort of like the fondue phase she went through—that she'd bring out to impress her company. But I know she got the most enjoyment when she made this pie for Daddy on a weekday, because he liked it so much. You should have seen the glorious look on her face when he'd push away from the table and wink or blow a kiss, or make some quick, little gesture that he thought I didn't see, and say, "Supper *sho* was good."

½ cup light corn syrup

½ cup creamy peanut butter

4 cups crushed cereal flakes (I use Kellogg's Nut & Honey® cereal)

4 cups vanilla ice cream, slightly softened

¾ cup caramel dessert topping

¾ cup chopped salted peanuts

Makes one 9-inch pie

Butter a 9-inch pie plate and set aside.

In a small saucepan, heat the corn syrup just until it starts to boil, then remove from the heat and stir in the peanut butter and the crushed cereal until the flakes are well coated. Press the mixture evenly into the bottom and up the sides of the buttered pie plate. Put the plate in the freezer until the crust is firm, 10 to 15 minutes.

In a medium-size bowl, thoroughly blend together the ice cream, ½ cup of the caramel topping, and ½ cup of the peanuts. Spoon the mixture into the chilled crust. Sprinkle the remaining ¼ cup peanuts over the filling, pressing them into the surface. Drizzle the remaining ¼ cup caramel topping over the pie.

Place in the freezer until firm, about 4 hours. Remove 10 minutes before you plan to serve it to let it soften a bit to make slicing easier.

Laura Cullenbine's Rice Krispies® Pie

My walking time relieves my stress. When I am walking, locked into my own rhythm, breathing, and movement, and observing the situation around me—the trees, flowers, sky, birds, and other people—it becomes my medicine; walking clears my mind. But regardless of the exquisite peace and solitude that my solo walking jaunts provide, I prefer the half hour lunch walks that I take with my friend Laura. Our walks lead naturally to womanly conversations. Within that thirty-minute time frame, we expound on our lives: what we want, what we value, some of the things that we've been through. Somehow, being on the trail with another woman reveals itself as a source of power and alchemy; you laugh at things that you wouldn't ordinarily find funny, you confess things you wouldn't normally confess, and you remember things you thought you'd forgotten.

Laura tells me that while she was growing up, her mother was a meticulous housekeeper, whose immaculate kitchen was her pride and joy. Laura says because of her mother's desire to keep the kitchen spotless, it was pretty much off limits. Laura says that when she was growing up she loved to look at the pictures in her mother's cookbooks. She says she taught herself to cook that way. Says, late at night after everyone had gone to bed, she would sneak into her mother's gleaming kitchen and whip up the most enjoyable little meals. Of course, Laura was always mindful to leave her mother's kitchen in the meticulous condition in which she had found it.

Laura says she put this scrumptious pie together late one night—says she couldn't have been more than ten—and she's been making it ever since.

- 2 tablespoons unsalted butter, melted
- ¾ cup marshmallow creme (like Marshmallow Fluff®)
- 2½ cups Rice Krispies cereal
- 1 quart ice cream of your choice, slightly softened
- Ice cream topping of your choice

Makes one 9-inch deep-dish pie

Lightly butter a 9-inch deep-dish pie pan.

In a large bowl, blend together the melted butter, marshmallow creme, and Rice Krispies until well mixed. Evenly spread the mixture over the bottom and up the sides of the pie pan to form a crust. Fill the crust with the ice cream and freeze at least 6 hours.

Remove from the freezer, top with your favorite ice cream topping, and let soften 10 minutes to make slicing easier before serving.

Miss Eudora's Cream of Wheat® Custard Pie

When I was a little girl, my mother's seamstress friend, Miss Eudora Hawkins, was a sweet little bulldog of a woman. Despite her raspy voice and gruff exterior—sewing pins and darning needles growing out of the sides of her mouth like cat's whiskers—Miss Eudora was as sweet as grape jelly on the inside. Each time we stopped in for a visit, just before Miss Eudora whisked my mother off to her cramped little sewing room to examine swatches of fabric and new sewing techniques, Miss Eudora would turn to me and say, "Dearie, how would you like a nice little piece of pie?" Old-fashioned mincemeat or chocolate silk—she would always say the same thing: "You wait here, Dearie. I'm gonna fetch you a nice little piece of pie."

Miss Eudora's Cream of Wheat custard pie may sound odd, but there's nothing odd about the way it tastes. I especially like my slices served slightly warm with a dollop of home-whipped cream.

- One 9-inch single Flaky Pie Crust (page 8), rolled out, fitted into a pie plate, edge trimmed and crimped
- 2 cups whole milk
- ½ cup sugar
- ⅓ cup instant Cream of Wheat cereal
- 1 teaspoon vanilla extract
- 3 large eggs
- ⅛ teaspoon salt

Makes one 9-inch pie

Preheat the oven to 425 degrees. Prepare the pie crust and partially prebake. Set aside on a wire rack. Reduce the oven temperature to 350 degrees.

In a medium-size heavy saucepan, combine the milk and sugar. Bring to a boil over medium heat, then slowly sprinkle in the Cream of Wheat, stirring constantly. Continue to cook and stir over medium heat for about 3 minutes. Remove the saucepan from the heat and let cool, stirring occasionally. Stir in the vanilla.

Separate the egg yolks and the egg whites into medium-size bowls. Beat the egg yolks, one at a time, into the cooled Cream of Wheat mixture. Add the salt to the bowl containing the egg whites and beat with an electric mixer until stiff, shiny peaks form. Stir about one-third of the egg whites into the filling. Gently but thoroughly, fold in the remaining egg whites. Pour the filling into the pie crust, place in the oven, and bake until the crust turns a nice golden color, 35 to 40 minutes. The filling will puff up as it bakes, then settle back down as it cools. Let cool on a wire rack for a bit and serve slightly warm with vanilla ice cream or whipped cream.

Bernice Brock's Old-Fashioned Grits Pie

According to a tale often told in my family, Sister Bernice Brock, a tall, plain-looking church woman who was as sweet as cherry pudding, had her sights set on Brother Varney, a confirmed bachelor, who got a kick out of entertaining the single ladies: taking them to the movies and out for long walks around Ojibway Island in Saginaw. It wasn't that Brother Varney was a playboy, it's just that he delighted in the lavish perks that went along with being an eligible bachelor in a congregation full of single women. Every Sunday, one sister or another was grinning in his face and saying, "I've got a little supper fixed at the house, why don't you stop by after service?"

Well, they tell me that instead of letting the situation depress her, for an entire year Bernice laid back like a fox, watching and listening and trying to learn as much about Brother Varney as she could; say she wanted to know his favorite ball team, the kind of car he would drive if suddenly he came into a bit of money, and whether he preferred his toilet paper with the flap on top or at the bottom.

There soon came a time, though, when one of Brother Varney's eccentricities came to the surface and outshone the others. With Bernice watching him like a hawk, she caught on to it right away—Brother Varney loved feet; in particular, his own.

Sister Bernice arrived at the sanctuary looking like an angel from heaven in a beautiful lavender suit and a matching wide-brimmed hat and high-heeled pumps.

Bernice, who by now had inched her way to the front pew where Brother Varney sat in the deacon's row facing her, had the perfect view. She watched Brother Varney sneaking quick, admiring glimpses at his feet; she saw the way he grimaced if he noticed even the tiniest speck or smudge on his shoe. She recognized the superb quality of his silk stockings. She came to see that the fine linen handkerchiefs sticking out of his suit pockets weren't there to wipe his brow, but rather to keep his shoes immaculate. When he thought no one was looking, Bernice would see him slide his dainty little feet out of their soft, alligator or lamb's skin encasements (his shoes looked more like ballerina slippers than men's shoes). He would twinkle his toes, smile tenderly, then quietly slide them back in.

With this new insight, you can imagine how hopeful Bernice felt when the church announced that it was going to have its first foot-washing ceremony. In John's gospel, as a symbol of brotherhood and humility, Jesus washed His disciples' feet immediately after the Last Supper. Although they are not very common today, foot-washing ceremonies were prevalent in many churches—from Roman Catholic to Southern Pentecostal—during the 1960s.

They say, Bernice, who normally was as quiet as a paper napkin, let out a whopping "Halleluiah!" They say, somehow, she managed to persuade "the foot-washing committee" to pair her with Brother Varney; say she went home and promptly read everything that she could find about pedicures, and foot massages—about feet in general. They tell me that on the day of the foot washing, Sister Bernice arrived at the sanctuary looking like an angel from Heaven; said she had on a beautiful lavender suit—Brother Varney's favorite color—and a matching, wide-brimmed hat and high-heeled pumps. They say she was carrying her own little foot tub and a paper sack full of sweet-smelling herbs and spices. Of course, since nobody could actually see inside the cloudy, herb-filled water, it's anybody's guess what Sister Bernice's hands were doing to Brother Varney's sensitive feet. But, you know people and how they'll talk, so it's at this point that the story tends to vary according to the recollections of the one who's telling it. Some say you could tell by the look on his face and from the unholy sounds escaping involuntarily from somewhere deep inside of him that Sister Bernice was giving Brother Varney a foot washing unlike any other. So much so that after the ceremony the deacons and the elders promptly came together and decided to put an end to all subsequent foot-washing ceremonies. Said they didn't want to have a part in something that had the potential to swing too far away from its Holy significance. They say, a few Sundays later, Sister Bernice came to church wearing the prettiest band of engagement diamonds that you'd ever want to see. Of course, to those who asked Sister Brock outright—and many did—if it were true that it was her foot-washing skills that enabled her to extract a marriage proposal out of a steadfast bachelor like Brother Varney, she promptly answered no. She said it was his love of grits; said he loved eating grits more than anything. Some declare it was the foot washing; others side with Sister Brock and say it was the grits pie that lured Brother Varney down the aisle.

- One 9-inch single Flaky Pie Crust (page 8), rolled out, fitted into a pie plate, and edge trimmed and crimped
- 1 cup quick-cooking grits, cooked according to package instructions and cooled slightly
- 1¼ cups firmly packed dark brown sugar
- 2½ teaspoons all-purpose flour
- 2 large eggs, lightly beaten
- ¼ cup milk
- 3 tablespoons unsalted butter, melted
- 1½ teaspoons vanilla extract
- 1 teaspoon distilled white vinegar

Makes one 9-inch pie

Preheat the oven to 350 degrees. Prepare the crust and set aside.

In a good-size bowl, combine the grits, brown sugar, flour, and eggs until well mixed. Stir in the milk and butter, then the vanilla and vinegar. Pour the filling into the pie crust. Place in the oven and bake until the center is just set, 35 to 40 minutes. Let cool slightly on a wire rack. Serve while the pie is still warm. I usually serve this pie topped with vanilla ice cream or homemade whipped topping, but it tastes just as good plain.

Miss Mancini's Rice Pie

Miss Mancini, a meticulous little Italian woman, owned the tidy little store that stood on the corner at the end of our street. She lived a couple of houses away from us in a tall and meticulously kept white house. I don't remember the name of her store, but I do remember that it was made of wood and painted a deep tomato red. It had a forest green awning over the plate-glass window in front and a little bell rang each time you entered or exited the store.

Miss Mancini sold her own home-baked breads, cakes, and pies in the store, and even though we all knew that she wouldn't give out her recipes, that didn't stop the women in my family from asking. Cousin Sarah Jane, my grandmother's cousin from Mississippi, came to visit one summer. After buying one of Miss Mancini's rice pies, Cousin Sarah Jane *had* to have the recipe. The next time Sarah Jane saw Miss Mancini she said, "I hate to tell you this, because everyone around here speaks so highly of your cooking, but I was a might disappointed in that rice pie I bought from you the other day. Where I come from, folks *really* know how to make a good rice pie." They say Miss Mancini took offense immediately and wanted to know what was wrong with her rice pie and how she could fix it. Cousin Sarah Jane, who was in her mid-seventies and still as quick as a fox said, "Well, you tell me what you're puttin' in your rice pies, and I'll tell you what you might be doin' wrong." My mother used to say, *Keep your eyes open; people have all kinds of ways of gettin' what they want from you.*

- One 9-inch single Flaky Pie Crust (page 8), rolled out, fitted into a pie plate, and edge trimmed and crimped
- 3 large eggs
- 1¼ cups sugar
- 1¾ cups ricotta cheese
- 1½ teaspoons fresh lemon juice
- 1½ teaspoons grated lemon rind
- 2 cups heavy cream
- ¼ cup cooked white rice
- ⅛ teaspoon ground cinnamon

Makes one 9-inch pie

Preheat the oven to 350 degrees. Prepare the pie crust and set aside.

Crack the eggs into a large bowl and beat until well blended. Beat in the sugar, then stir in the ricotta and lemon juice and rind until thoroughly incorporated. Add the cream and stir until smooth and creamy. Fold in the rice, then stir in the cinnamon. Pour the filling into the pie crust. Place in the oven and bake until a toothpick inserted in the center comes out clean and the top is nicely browned, 45 to 60 minutes. Let cool completely on a wire rack before serving.

The Egg Lady's Oatmeal Pie

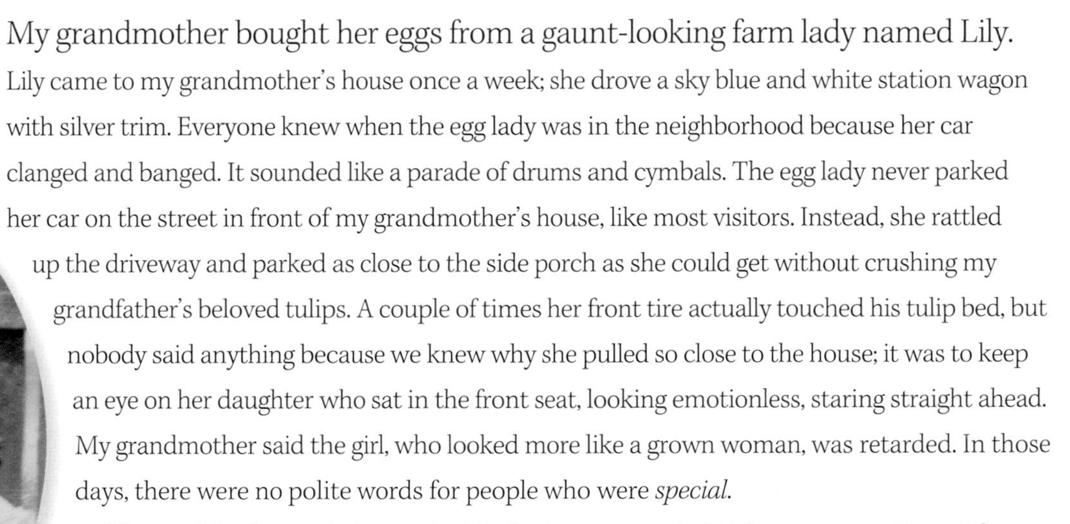

My grandmother bought her eggs from a gaunt-looking farm lady named Lily. Lily came to my grandmother's house once a week; she drove a sky blue and white station wagon with silver trim. Everyone knew when the egg lady was in the neighborhood because her car clanged and banged. It sounded like a parade of drums and cymbals. The egg lady never parked her car on the street in front of my grandmother's house, like most visitors. Instead, she rattled up the driveway and parked as close to the side porch as she could get without crushing my grandfather's beloved tulips. A couple of times her front tire actually touched his tulip bed, but nobody said anything because we knew why she pulled so close to the house; it was to keep an eye on her daughter who sat in the front seat, looking emotionless, staring straight ahead. My grandmother said the girl, who looked more like a grown woman, was retarded. In those days, there were no polite words for people who were *special*.

Often, while the egg lady was inside the house, rapt in kitchen conversation with my grandmother, I would ease out to the porch on the side yard and stare at the slow white girl. Simultaneously, I was in awe of her *and* I was afraid of her. Truth be told, I was even a little afraid of the egg lady. Most of the white women who came to my grandmother's neighborhood—schoolteachers, hat shop owners, and landlords dressed in fur coats—carried themselves with the poise of entitlement. To encounter one who wore tattered, flower-patterned housedresses and another, who had a slow, backward manner, was unsettling.

One day, my cousins (shown above) and I were in the side yard playing a circle game where everybody held hands. The egg lady and her daughter putted up the driveway and, for the first time, the egg lady coaxed her daughter out of the car to play with us. My cousins were warm and hospitable, but when the tall woman-girl stood next to me and reached out for my hand, I refused to give it to her. "Go on, Patty!" my little cousins insisted. "Take her hand." No matter how they pleaded or what they threatened, I wouldn't hold the retarded girl's hand. Eventually, the egg lady sent her daughter back to the car.

As soon as Lily and my grandmother finished their business, my grandmother called me in. "I'm surprised at you, Sug," she said. "I've never seen you act out like that. Why wouldn't you hold the girl's hand?" I didn't know what to say. The word "intolerance" wasn't in my vocabulary.

My grandmother sent me to a little red chair in the corner where I was to consider, "how would you feel if someone refused to hold your hand because you were different?" As soon as I received enlightenment, I was to let my grandmother know, then I could rejoin my cousins outside.

I experienced no revelations that day. I was a little girl, blinded by family love and community acceptance. A lack of experience made it impossible for me to ponder the thought of ever being judged or rejected because I wasn't the answer to somebody's standard. Years later, I wish I could tell my grandmother and the egg lady's daughter how sorry I am for acting out that day. If I could, I would tell the egg lady's daughter, "Now that I've been out in the world, I know how it feels to be misunderstood. I know how it feels to stretch your hand out, and have it rejected: it doesn't feel good. Please forgive me . . . I'm sorry, I'm sorry, I'm so sorry."

The egg lady sold pies out of the back of her station wagon. My grandmother said she sold eggs and pies to make ends meet. She said Hubert Len, the egg lady's husband, was one of those kinds of husbands who leave the house and head for the corner store, "and you don't know whether they'll be back in six minutes or in six months." Hubert Len was what my grandmother called *a rambling man*, a man who couldn't "stay put" for very long.

Like Hubert Len, the oatmeal called for in the egg lady's pie recipe doesn't stay put either. It rises to the top and forms a crunchy top crust. It is a simple pie that will surprise you.

One 9-inch single Flaky Pie Crust (page 8), rolled out, fitted into a pie plate, and edge trimmed and crimped

2 large eggs

¼ cup (½ stick) unsalted butter, melted

1 teaspoon vanilla extract

⅔ cup sugar

⅔ cup light corn syrup

⅔ cup old-fashioned oats

Makes one 9-inch pie

Preheat the oven to 350 degrees. Prepare the pie crust and set aside.

In a medium-size bowl, beat the eggs. Add the butter, vanilla, sugar, and corn syrup and stir until well mixed. Fold in the oats until well blended, then pour the mixture into the crust.

Place in the oven and bake until the crust is golden brown and the filling firm to the touch, about 45 minutes. Let cool on a wire rack 15 to 20 minutes before serving.

4

Cream & Custard Pies

More than anyone, my mother influenced my understanding of the power and magic of a cooking woman. Mama, who had a beautiful figure and a gorgeous face, wasn't wrapped up in her looks. She would put herself together in the morning (gathering her hair into a ponytail and applying a dash of red lipstick). As I recall, she didn't go back to the mirror until it was almost time for Daddy to come home, when she would put on something crisp, let down her hair, and apply more lipstick.

Instead of putting emphasis on makeup and lavish hairstyles, Mama expressed herself through her cooking skills. When we were in the kitchen together, she would say wise things like "Don't put your spoon in a pot that won't boil for you," "A man doesn't wander far from where the pot is boiling," or "A slice of good custard pie will perk up anybody."

Like Mama, I don't do a lot of primping. I own a tube or two of red lipstick, and several wands of mascara; that's all. And that's why I like cream and custard pies; they're so uncomplicated.

Susan Howell's Banana Coconut Tarts

My good friend Susan tells me that she cooks every meal as though that particular meal will be the one her boyfriend, Edward, will always remember her for. She says it picks her up when Edward, who's normally not much of an eater asks, "Got any more of that?" Susan says she relishes the compliments she receives for her cooking skills, the way some women like to hear how good they look in their hair and makeup. According to Susan, her banana coconut tarts always garner a rave review from Edward; and that's why she makes them every chance she gets.

For some women, cooking for a man is more than just a matter of throwing something together and saying, "eat this"; it's about tailoring what they cook (adding the extra shredded cheese, omitting the bell peppers, or substituting one flavor for another) to please his palate. It's about pouring a measure of themselves into what they cook—ultimately, offering him servings of love and passion on his supper plate.

When you put that kind of ardor into your cooking, it's no more than right to expect the man you're cooking for to show a little appreciation.

¼ cup (½ stick) unsalted butter, softened

1 cup sugar

1 large egg, slightly beaten

½ cup milk

1 ripe banana, peeled and mashed

1½ cups sweetened shredded coconut

Dough for one 9-inch single Flaky Pie Crust (page 8)

Makes twelve 3- to 4-inch tarts

Preheat the oven to 350 degrees.

In a medium-size bowl, beat the butter and sugar together until light and creamy. Beat in the egg, milk, and banana until smooth. Stir in 1 cup of the coconut.

On a lightly floured work surface, roll out the dough until ⅛ inch thick. Cut the dough into 12 circles about 1 inch larger than the mini tart pans (or you can use a muffin tins) you will be using. Line the pans or tins with the circles of dough and trim the edges even with the top of the pan.

Spoon the filling into the shells and bake until the tarts are a light toasty brown, about 20 minutes. Susan says she starts checking for doneness after 10 minutes. During the last 5 minutes of baking time, sprinkle the remaining ½ cup coconut on a cookie sheet, put it in the oven with the tarts, and let brown, watching so it doesn't burn. When the coconut is toasted, about 5 minutes, take it out of the oven. Take the tarts out of the oven and sprinkle the coconut on top of each one. Let cool completely on a wire rack before serving.

Carlean's Sweet Potato-Coconut Custard Pie

3½ cups water

3 large sweet potatoes, peeled and sliced about ¼ inch thick

Dough for one 9 x 13-inch double Flaky Pie Crust (page 8)

1 cup plus 4 teaspoons granulated sugar

½ cup firmly packed dark brown sugar

3 tablespoons all-purpose flour

1 teaspoon grated orange rind

½ teaspoon ground nutmeg

⅛ teaspoon salt

1½ cups sweetened shredded coconut

¼ cup orange juice

½ cup (1 stick) unsalted butter, cubed

2 tablespoons unsalted butter, melted

Makes one 9 x 13-inch pie

Before Miss Carlean sauntered into our small town and opened up her glamorous little beauty parlor, most of us had never seen a woman quite that exotic. Miss Carlean, a former "Fiesta Dancer" at the famous Paradise Club in Idlewild, Michigan, put you in the mind of a bronze-colored Sophia Loren. Idlewild, once referred to as the Black Eden, was the most prestigious African American resort community in the United States in the 1950s and 1960s.

They tell me jealous wives and girlfriends set off all kinds of nasty little rumors about Miss Carlean, just to taint the fascination that most of us had with her. In fact, I was in line once, standing behind two surly looking women when Miss Carlean switched by; I heard one of the women say, "Hmmp. She may be nice looking but I bet she can't keep house," to which the other woman replied, "Bet she can't cook neither—women like that usually can't."

My mother used to say, *You can't stop talk.*

As it turned out, Miss Carlean and I became wonderful friends. And I'm here to tell you, not only can she keep house, she's a splendid cook, as well. Above all, I like her rich baking.

Preheat the oven to 350 degrees.

Pour the water into a large Dutch oven or saucepan and bring to a boil. Add the sweet potatoes and cook until almost tender, about 10 minutes.

While the sweet potatoes are cooking, divide the pie dough into two balls, one slightly larger than the other. On a lightly floured work surface, roll out the larger piece into a 12 x 16-inch rectangle (about 1½ inches beyond the edge of an inverted 9 x 13-inch baking dish). Fit the bottom crust into the dish. Trim the edge even with the top edge of the dish and prick the bottom with a fork. Place in the oven and bake for 5 minutes. Remove from the oven and set aside.

Drain the sweet potatoes, reserving 1 cup of the cooking water. Spread the potatoes evenly over the prebaked crust. Pour the reserved cooking water over the potatoes.

In a medium-size bowl, combine 1 cup of the granulated sugar, all the brown sugar, flour, orange rind, nutmeg, salt, coconut, and orange juice until well mixed. Pour evenly over the sweet potatoes. Dot the filling with the cubes of butter.

Roll out the remaining ball of dough into a 10 x 14-inch rectangle that extends about ½ inch beyond the edge of the baking dish. Cover the filling with the top crust. Seal the edges by pressing them together with the tines of a fork. Cut slits in the top crust, brush with the melted butter, and sprinkle with the remaining 4 teaspoons granulated sugar. Place in the oven and bake until the crust is golden brown, 40 to 45 minutes. Let cool for a few minutes on a wire rack before serving warm, with a tall glass of milk.

I heard one of the women say, "Hmmp. She may be nice looking but I bet she can't keep house," to which the other woman replied, "Bet she can't cook neither—women like that usually can't."

Frankie's Coconut Pie

When I was a little girl, my parents turned the upstairs of our two-story home into an apartment that they rented to a succession of interesting tenants. One of the most colorful families to live above us was a woman named Frankie and her run-around husband, Lewis.

Frankie was a tall, dark-skinned woman with a skinny, boyish frame, and Lewis was petite, with big, pearly teeth, and jet-black, wavy hair—he brought Cab Calloway to mind. My grandmother used to say he was a shameless, middle-aged playboy who needed to go somewhere and sit down. But my mother would say, "It takes some men longer than others to run their race out, before they're ready to come in out of the streets."

Frankie and Lewis used to have the most volatile arguments. Once, my father opened the living room door that led to the apartment and yelled up the stairs, "Will y'all please keep it down?" Frankie yelled back down the stairs, "And would you please mind your own damn business!?"

Frankie had a mouth. When they got started, she kept up with Lewis, word for word. One time, while my parents were sound asleep, I heard Lewis tiptoeing up the back stairs just outside my bedroom window. It was early in the morning. The door opened upstairs and no sooner than it did, Frankie said, "You ain't foolin' nobody, leastwise not me! Talkin' 'bout you just left the pool hall. This ain't New York City; this is Saginaw, Michigan. There ain't nothin' open in this city, this time 'a morning, 'cept some loose woman's legs!"

When I inherited my mother's massive, handwritten recipe collection, one of the first entrees that I came across was a recipe with these words inscribed above it: Frankie: One hard woman, but a really good cook. This pie of hers makes its own crust, with the coconut rising to the top.

3 large eggs
1 cup sugar
2 cups whole milk
½ cup (1 stick) unsalted butter, melted
½ cup all-purpose flour
1 teaspoon vanilla extract
1 cup sweetened shredded coconut

Makes one 9- or 10-inch pie

Preheat the oven to 350 degrees.

Crack the eggs, one at a time, into a large bowl and mix until well blended. Add the sugar, milk, melted butter, and flour and mix until well blended. Pour in the vanilla, add the coconut, and mix well. Pour into a 9- or 10-inch pie plate, place in the oven, and bake until the center feels firm, 50 to 55 minutes. Let cool completely on a wire rack before serving with whipped cream.

Sister Baby's Buttermilk Pie

They tell me that Mama's cousin Sister Baby was a real contradiction in womanhood. Sister Baby, who started in the fast lane early (they say, by the time Sister was twelve, Cousin Rachel, her mother, couldn't do a thing with her), was one of those kind of girls who could get out there and revel with the best of them. But, after she'd had enough carousing, she could step inside, slip into one of Cousin Rachel's nice aprons, and cook a meal so tasty, it was hard to believe Sister cooked it. They say, her pies would come out of the oven looking like a picture.

Sister kept a string of male admirers. Of course, some in the family say Sister attracted men so easily because of her fastness; others say it was because of her cooking. I don't know what drew the men to Sister, the fact that she was a party girl or the notion that when she put her mind to it, she was a wonderful cook. I do know that even though my mother used to preach her "fast-girls-end-up-going-nowhere" sermon, she also used to say, "But it won't get you anywhere being too slow either."

- One 9-inch single Flaky Pie Crust (page 8), rolled out, fitted into a pie plate, and edge trimmed and crimped
- 1¼ cups sugar
- ½ cup (1 stick) unsalted butter, softened
- 3 large eggs, slightly beaten
- 3 tablespoons all-purpose flour
- 1 cup buttermilk
- 1 teaspoon vanilla extract
- 1 teaspoon lemon extract

Makes one 9-inch pie

Preheat the oven to 350 degrees. Prepare the pie crust and set aside.

In a medium-size bowl, cream together the sugar, butter, and eggs. Beat in the flour. Stir in the buttermilk until well mixed. Stir in the extracts. Pour the filling into the pie crust, place in the oven, and bake until the filling is golden brown and still has a little wiggle to it, 40 to 45 minutes. Let cool completely on a wire rack before serving.

Miss Bradley's Cottage Cheese Pie

Miss Bradley was the kind of woman who walked the streets all times of day and night looking for her daughter Jewel. "Y'all seen Jewel? Jewel been this way?" The sight of Miss Bradley, anxiously searching the streets for her wild-child, Jewel, stood out, even on busy 6th Street—my grandmother's street—where a steady stream of odd traffic flowed by, day and night. On late summer evenings when Miss Bradley scurried worriedly by my grandmother's front porch, we all felt sorry for her—even us kids who didn't quite know what it was that we were feeling sorry for.

You see, there were two sides to 6th Street when I was growing up; one end was conducive to church going and family raising. It hosted a series of family-owned businesses, churches and community centers, beauty and barber shops, a Catholic school and a funeral parlor. It was the family-friendly end of the long and winding street.

There was nothing family-friendly about the other end of the street. Even though the same sun shone equally on both ends of the street, the bad end, with its dimly lit bars and rowdy pool halls, its dubious street corners, and the pretty girls who stood on them, posing like movie stars and fashion models, always looked gloomy. Decent folk didn't walk toward the bad end after dark.

Sometimes, shortly after the street lights came on and we were sitting comfortably on my grandmother's front porch, sipping sodas and talking about the people passing by, we could see Jewel Bradley sauntering our way, walking against the flow of good girls who were heading

Everybody in the neighborhood kept an eye on Miss Bradley's was on the wrong path

toward their homes at the good end of the street. Jewel stood out, not just because the street lights were popping on and she was headed toward the bad end, but also because everybody in the neighborhood kept an eye on Miss Bradley's pretty young daughter Jewel, who everybody prophesied was on the wrong path and headed for trouble. The folks in the neighborhood shook their heads and said, "Uh, uh, uh, po' Miss Bradley," when she scurried past their porches asking, "You seen Jewel? Jewel been this way?"

Jewel, who was a light-skinned girl with big, juicy, ruby-red lips, a big, juicy behind, and big, juicy legs, wore tight skirts and tight sweaters that clung to the curves of her juicy body like heat clings to the sun. To a little girl like me, a big, brassy girl like Jewel Bradley seemed invincible. She would strut by my grandmother's porch, her head cocked defiantly, without speaking. In those days it was considered rude to walk by a porch without speaking to its occupants; only the most confident, the most insolent, had the courage to do such a thing. When she walked by late in the evening, going the opposite way of the good girls, popping her gum like a firecracker, switching like a cat in heat, and dragging a trail of loud, dime-store perfume, I thought she was really going somewhere. When my grandmother wasn't looking, I'd mark Jewel's progress until she was way up the street. I used to think, when I grow up I'm gonna walk like Jewel Bradley, crack my gum like Jewel Bradley, and venture to the bad end of 6th Street like Jewel Bradley. But then, my grandmother who was always reading my mind, would quietly say, "That girl's on the wrong path, Sug. She's headed for trouble." And then, as if to drive the point home, no sooner was Jewel was out of sight than a worried looking Miss Bradley would come hurrying up the street, asking all the folks who were sitting on their porches trying to catch the last drop of cool breeze before they turned into their hot houses for the night, "Y'all seen Jewel? Jewel been this way?"

pretty young daughter Jewel, who everybody prophesied and headed for trouble.

Everybody in our neighborhood liked Miss Bradley; she was a real sweety pie. She would cook up a bunch of stuff, then pass it around the neighborhood by way of her well-behaved daughter Ritas. Ritas wasn't big and juicy like Jewel; she was thin and dry and quieter. She was the dutiful daughter everyone upheld as "Miss Bradley's consolation for all the heartache that Jewel's put her through."

When somebody that she knew was torn between two pursuits, my grandmother used to say, "You can't serve two masters, 'cause you may do well by one, but surely you'll neglect the other." Considering that Miss Bradley spent so much time in the streets (pursuing her wild-child, Jewel), we marveled at what a fine a cook she was. I especially liked the cottage cheese pies that she sent around; they put me in the mind of cheesecake, which I love.

- One 9-inch single Flaky Pie Crust (page 8), rolled out, fitted into a pie plate, and edge trimmed and crimped
- 2 cups small curd cottage cheese
- ½ cup to ¾ cup sugar, depending on how sweet you want the pie
- One 3-ounce package instant vanilla custard or pudding mix
- 2 tablespoons unsalted butter, melted
- ¾ cup evaporated milk
- 1½ teaspoons vanilla extract
- 2 large eggs, separated
- ¼ teaspoon ground nutmeg
- Pinch of salt

Makes one 9-inch pie

Prepare the pie crust and set aside.

Empty the cottage cheese into a strainer and let it set over a bowl in the refrigerator until most of the liquid has drained away; this takes about 1 hour. Then, preheat the oven to 350 degrees.

In a large bowl, combine the drained cottage cheese, sugar, custard mix, and melted butter and mix well. Stir in the milk, vanilla, egg yolks, nutmeg, and salt until thoroughly combined.

In a medium-size bowl, beat the egg whites with an electric mixer until they hold firm peaks when the beaters are lifted out. Fold them into yolk mixture until there are no more white streaks. Pour the filling into the pie crust. Place in the oven and bake until a knife inserted in the center comes out clean, about 45 minutes. The pie should be firm, not runny. Let cool completely on a wire rack before serving. In my opinion, this is one of those pies that taste better the next day.

Frida's Lemon Chess Pie

When I was twelve, Frida, a wonderful matronly neighbor, taught me a tremendous lesson on how to handle womanly setbacks. When Frida's handsome, flirtatious husband Garfield, left her, even though she was heartbroken she did not sit at home with a bottle of gin. She quickly reinvented herself as a modern, single woman. Truth be told, she put herself together quite well. She bought new shoes, new dresses, a new perfume, false eyelashes, and a new wig. They say, Frida was so nicely transformed that it startled Garfield; say he didn't recognize his own wife of twenty years when he started bumping into her in the lounges around town.

They say other men began saying such nice things to Frida like "Where you been hidin' out, gorgeous? . . . I must have died and gone straight to heaven, cause you sho' look like an angel to me." She soon developed an air of superiority. They say she'd point her nose in the air and walk right past Garfield (in the supermarket or at the post office) like she'd never seen the man. She'd greet him in church with an obligatory, holy kind of handshake that didn't come close to the liveliness with which she started shaking the other men's hands. They say you could have bought high and mighty Garfield with a wooden nickel, he was so outdone.

My mother used to say, *A man hates to be ignored.*

When Garfield saw how easily Frida was moving on without him, he soon commenced to begging his way back home. Frida declared, "Under one condition, and one condition only . . . all these years you've been gettin' by the bushel but giving by the spoon. From now on, I'm not gonna do all the giving, and you ain't gonna do all the getting. If we can come to the same mind on that, I'd be glad to have you come back home."

Frida declared, "... all these years you've been gettin' by the bushel but giving by the spoon. From now on, I'm not gonna do all the giving, and you ain't gonna do all the getting."

That was all that needed to be said. Garfield was a better man when he went back home. He was still a little stuck on himself—arrogance was just in his nature—but now he wasn't quite as prissy. You could pass by the house on any given day and see him working in the yard or climbing up a ladder, engrossed in some other manly chore around the place.

As for Frida, she cautiously changed back into the homebody that we had always admired. Eventually, she boxed up her new clothes and wig and sent them around the corner to Sister Ulaine McKnight, whose husband, Horace, had started acting the fool.

Truth be told, everybody was glad when Frida transformed herself back because the other Frida, the new, modern Frida didn't spend much time in the kitchen. We missed the wonderful desserts that she used to pass around, especially this lovely lemon chess pie.

- One 9-inch single Flaky Pie Crust (page 8), rolled out, fitted into a pie plate, with pinched edge rim (see directions)
- ½ cup (1 stick) unsalted butter, softened
- 1½ cups sugar
- 1½ tablespoons yellow cornmeal
- 3 large eggs
- 3 tablespoons fresh lemon juice
- 2 teaspoons grated lemon rind
- 1 teaspoon vanilla extract
- ⅛ teaspoon salt

Makes one 9-inch pie

Preheat the oven to 350 degrees. Prepare the pie crust and set aside.

In a large bowl, cream together the butter and sugar until well blended. Stir in the cornmeal. Beat in the eggs, one at a time. Add the lemon juice and rind, vanilla, and salt and blend well.

Retrieve your pie crust. Use your thumb and index finger to pinch the edge of the crust all the way around the pie. Using a fork, press down into the dough, moving around the entire rim of the pie. Do not press all the way through the dough. To doll up the crust a little more, crisscross the markings at a 45-degree angle by pressing the fork down with its tines pointing to the left, then rotate the pie slightly, and press down with the tines pointing to the right.

Pour the filling into the pie crust, place in the oven, and bake until a knife inserted in the center comes out clean, 35 to 40 minutes. Let cool completely on a wire rack before serving.

Mary Lawrence's Peaches and Cream Pie

My good friend Mary Lawrence is a petite, well-dressed woman whose chic outfits remind me of the kind of elegant ensembles that Edith Head designed for Hollywood's elite actresses like Barbara Stanwyck and Audrey Hepburn.

Mary is the features and food writer for *The Saginaw News*. When she and I go out (Mary gets invited to everything), she is the kind of woman who wears a three-quarter length mink and matching hat, and a tangerine-colored slip dress with tangerine-colored slippers to match. You know a woman is a real dresser when she has a closet full of shoes that match every color in her wardrobe.

Mary acquired this scrumptious pie recipe from her cousin's husband, Michael, who invited her to supper one evening, determined to impress her with his cooking. Mary enjoyed the meal, and especially this pie, which she's been cooking ever since.

¾ cup self-rising flour

One 3-ounce box vanilla pie pudding mix (the cook-and-serve kind, not instant)

3 tablespoons unsalted butter, melted

1 large egg

½ cup milk

One 29-ounce can sliced peaches, drained (reserve 3 tablespoons of syrup)

One 8-ounce package cream cheese, softened

1 cup sugar

1 tablespoon ground cinnamon

Makes one 9-inch deep-dish pie

Preheat the oven to 350 degrees. Grease a 9-inch deep-dish pie plate and set aside.

In a large bowl, mix together the flour, pudding mix, melted butter, egg, and milk until smooth. Pour the mixture into the prepared pie plate and arrange the sliced peaches on top.

In a medium-size bowl, using an electric mixer, beat together the cream cheese, reserved syrup, and ¾ cup of the sugar until well blended, then spread on top of the peaches.

Mix together the remaining ¼ cup sugar and the cinnamon in a small bowl and sprinkle evenly over the top of the pie. Place in the oven and bake until a knife inserted in the center comes out clean, 30 to 35 minutes. Let cool completely on a wire rack before serving.

As far as I'm concerned, this pie doesn't need a bit of embellishment to make it taste good.

Mama's Peach Custard Pie

My mother was a homebody. She loved to cook and clean and read and tend to her vegetable garden. She prepared homemade soaps, candles, and incense sticks in the kitchen sink, and then she'd pass them out as gifts. Except for Evonce Nickelberry, who worked the night shift at a downtown hamburger grill, my mother's girlfriends were also homebodies.

That's why it surprised the women in my family when Mama took such a liking to Miss Flora Patterson, a stylish, older, big-city woman, who moved to our small town on the insistence of her husband, Sonny. He was a native of Saginaw, who convinced Miss Flora that what our little town lacked in sophistication and grandeur it more than made up for in down-home hospitality. Everybody wondered what Mama, an Earth Mother type, saw in such an elaborate woman like Flora Patterson, who wore gloves and hats, and wasted no time in assembling a group of creamy socialites whom she skimmed from the top of Saginaw's high society. Mama didn't drink cocktails, she didn't smoke, and she didn't play the fancy card games that Miss Patterson and her jet-set crowd played. On the outside looking in, Mama seemed to be an anomaly in their midst, an outcast. Mama cooked everything from scratch, hung her wash outside in the fresh air, and she still starched and ironed her sheets and pillowcases; Miss Patterson and her fancy friends contracted out most of their domesticity.

On the outside looking in, Mama—the small town homemaker, and Flora—the big-city socialite—were ill-matched friends; but viewing it from the inside, if you were privy to one of the noon suppers that Mama hosted for Flora, and Flora's creamy friends, Rhea, Elsie, Juditha, and Lucille, you quickly saw that the admiration was mutual. Mama enjoyed the socialites

Mama cooked everything from scratch, hung her wash outside in the fresh air, and she still starched and ironed her sheets and pillowcases; Miss Patterson and her fancy friends contracted out most of their domesticity.

because of their conversations about books, movies, and travel, and, truth be told, Mama just liked a little upper crust decorum every now and then. That's what made her so interesting—she liked a little bit of everything. The socialites admired Mama's hospitality and her scratch-cooking—especially her peach custard pies. You should have heard the socialites cackling and carrying on while Mama set one of her homemade pies on the table in front of them—much of their high-class decorum flew right out the window.

- One 9-inch single Flaky Pie Crust (page 8), rolled out, fitted into a pie plate, and edge trimmed and crimped
- 3 tablespoons firmly packed brown sugar
- 5 tablespoons all-purpose flour
- 5 medium-size ripe peaches, peeled, pitted, and sliced
- One 12-ounce can evaporated milk
- 1 large egg, slightly beaten
- 1 teaspoon vanilla extract
- ⅔ cup granulated sugar
- ½ teaspoon ground cinnamon
- ¼ teaspoon ground nutmeg
- ⅛ teaspoon ground cloves

Makes one 9-inch pie

Preheat the oven to 425 degrees. Prepare the pie crust and set aside.

Combine the brown sugar and 3 tablespoons of the flour in a small bowl. Sprinkle evenly over the bottom of the pie crust. Arrange the peaches in the crust.

In a medium-size bowl, whisk together the evaporated milk, egg, and vanilla, then pour over the peaches. In a small bowl, combine the remaining 2 tablespoons flour, the granulated sugar, and spices and sprinkle over the top of the pie. Place in the oven and bake until a knife inserted in the center comes out clean, 45 to 50 minutes. Let cool completely on a wire rack before slicing. A dollop of vanilla ice cream with each serving tastes nice.

Sister Shirley Woods' Navy Bean Custard Pie

When I was growing up, Mama talked a lot about beans. Said, when she was a little girl, her mother's younger sister, Aunt Evelyn, made the most flavorsome bean soup; said it was chockful of meat and heat. Mama said when they came North, out of a financial precaution, my grandmother, who could extend a dollar from one month to the next, cooked so many bean suppers that, to this day, Aunt Marjell won't let a bean touch her lips.

Mama used to tell me, "If times ever get hard for you, stock up on beans. A person can live off beans if they have to—they stretch 'cause they're filling, and they taste better the next day." Even now, I always keep a bag of dried beans around the house—just in case.

If there ever comes a time where I have to eat beans for a spell, I'm glad I have Sister Shirley's bean pie recipe. At least that'll give me a delicious alternative every now and then.

- One 9-inch single Flaky Pie Crust (page 8), rolled out, fitted into a pie plate, and edge trimmed and crimped
- ¼ cup (½ stick) unsalted butter, softened
- 1½ cups mashed cooked navy beans
- ¾ cup sugar
- ½ cup evaporated milk
- ½ teaspoon vanilla extract
- 3 large eggs, lightly beaten
- ½ teaspoon ground nutmeg

Makes one 9-inch pie

Preheat the oven to 350 degrees. Prepare the pie crust and set aside.

In a large bowl, mix together the butter, beans, sugar, and evaporated milk until well blended. Add the vanilla, eggs, and nutmeg and mix until well combined. Pour the filling into the pie crust, place in the oven, and bake until a knife inserted in the center comes out clean, 50 to 60 minutes.

Sister Shirley serves each slice warm, with a scoop of whipped cream.

Ava Joy's Peanut Butter Cream Pie

Ava Joy Malone may not have been a Hollywood movie star, but in our small town she stopped traffic. She was shapely, her cat-shaped eyes were dark and piercing, and her short, jet-black hair was sleek and always in place. Ava Joy had flawless, nut-brown skin—the kind that reveals specks of gold and copper when the sun shines on it.

It wasn't easy being beautiful. The men—even good men like Deacon Swank, who confessed in church (two Sundays in a row!) that he'd given into temptation when he bumped into Ava Joy at Meat City and asked her if she wanted a ride home, knowing full well congeniality wasn't on his mind—often avoided her. That's because an encounter with Ava left an impression on their faces that they couldn't hide; they didn't feel like putting up with the grief their wives and girlfriends were going to give them when they got home. And the women, they had a love-hate relationship with Ava. They'd grin in her face and no sooner did she turn her back than they'd start picking her apart: "That dress is tolerable but them Salvation Army–lookin' shoes have got to go."

I came to know Ava Joy quite well, despite our age difference. When I turned ten, my mother paid Ava to show me how to make beaded jewelry. My crowning moments inside Miss Ava's house didn't come while we were sorting through the gorgeous beads that she kept in a huge glass jar. Rather, they were on those occasions when I arrived for my lessons early and found her in her kitchen, all decked out in earrings and a dress, nylons and high heels, red lipstick and perfume. The people in the neighborhood could say what they wanted to say about Miss Ava Joy Malone, but to me, when she was sauntering around in her kitchen, all

made-up like a Hollywood movie star, that's when she was in her glory. Her femininity and softness mesmerized me.

My mother had strict rules for me, but when it came to lessons in womanhood, she was exceptionally broadminded. I'm glad she understood that being in the company of a woman like Miss Ava Joy Malone was a necessary aspect of my education. I'm glad Mama understood that when a young girl is in the kitchen with a womanly woman like Miss Ava Joy, the young girl envisions herself in all of her womanish possibilities, inside of a kitchen and out.

All these years later, whenever I make this pie, I see Miss Ava moving around in her kitchen—the way she slinked around in those high, high heels and the way she would close her refrigerator door with a tap of her hip. I remember a special moment when she asked me to stir her pots while she went to get her purse to pay the paper boy. When she came back to the kitchen, for a moment she looked at me with those dark, cat eyes and then she said, "You look like you're gonna grow up and be a good little cook."

- One 9-inch single Flaky Pie Crust (page 8), rolled out, fitted into a pie plate, and edge trimmed and scalloped (see directions)
- 1 cup chunky peanut butter
- 1 teaspoon vanilla extract
- ¼ teaspoon salt
- 2 tablespoons unsalted butter, melted
- 3 large eggs
- 1 cup dark corn syrup
- ⅔ cup sugar

Makes one 9-inch pie

Preheat the oven to 375 degrees. Prepare the pie crust and set aside.

In a medium-size bowl, using an electric mixer, beat together the peanut butter, vanilla, salt, and melted butter until well blended.

In a large bowl, beat the eggs, corn syrup, and sugar together with the mixer, then fold in the peanut butter mixture. When thoroughly combined, pour the filling into the pie crust.

To fashion an attractive scalloped edge around the pie, trim the dough even with the edge of the pie plate. Form a "V" with your right thumb and index finger about 1 inch apart. Place the "V" on the outside rim of the pie crust. Place your left index finger on the inside rim of the crust, inside the "V." Gently pinch your thumb and right forefinger, then press down your left forefinger inside the "V" on top of the mound of dough. Don't push all the way through the dough. Continue this pinch–press down, pattern around the rim of the pie.

Place the pie in the oven and bake until the crust is golden brown, 40 to 50 minutes. Let cool on a wire rack; it tastes good served still warm or chilled. Garnish with whipped cream.

Sister Chestermae Hayes's Apple Butter Pie

Mama knew the deal: that a man's home was supposed to feel like his castle. And believe me, Mama went out of her way to make Daddy feel sovereign. She would plate his food and bring it to the table; keep the pillows in his favorite chair plumped; and when he came home, dirty and tired, from his factory job at General Motors, she would run him a nice, hot bath. But when it came to the upkeep of the house, Mama didn't pacify Daddy; she urged him to pull his own weight. She prodded him to remove his work shoes at the door; to fold the newspaper and put it away, and to keep the trash from overflowing. Mama used to say, "If somebody comes by the house and catches it torn up, they won't be lookin' at you, they'll be lookin' at me." A man's house might be his castle, but people look to his wife to keep it intact.

My friend Chestermae Hayes, whose husband, Dr. Byron C. Hayes, pastors a thousand-member church (Word of Faith Ministries) in our small town, always tells me, "A wise woman builds her home every day."

Sister Hayes says there are many ways that a woman can build a sturdy house, but one of the best is to build it one good meal at a time. According to Sister Hayes, her scrumptious apple butter pie is one of the tools she uses.

- One 9-inch single deep-dish Flaky Pie Crust (page 8), rolled out, fitted into a pie plate, and edge trimmed and crimped
- 1½ cups apple butter
- ½ cup firmly packed dark brown sugar
- ¼ teaspoon salt
- ½ teaspoon ground cinnamon
- ½ teaspoon ground nutmeg
- 3 large eggs, slightly beaten
- 1 cup evaporated milk

Makes one 9-inch deep-dish pie

Preheat the oven to 350 degrees. Prepare the pie crust and set aside.

In a large bowl, thoroughly combine the apple butter, brown sugar, salt, cinnamon, and nutmeg. Stir in the eggs. Gradually add the evaporated milk, mixing well. Pour the filling into the pie crust, place in the oven, and bake until a knife inserted in the center comes out clean, 40 to 50 minutes. Let cool completely on a wire rack before serving with fresh whipped cream and pecan pieces or vanilla ice cream.

5

Fruit Pies

The old adage "even the best of friends must part" sums up something that happened the other night between me and one of my dearest girlfriends—I'll just call her Nay-Nay.

This is what happened. Nay-Nay called me and asked if I wanted to go out for coffee and pastries. She said, "If we have time, we'll stop off at the mall for a minute." In a small town, folks use the mall as much for socializing as they do for window shopping.

We got to the mall and start bumping into people that we knew. As soon as we finished grinning in someone's face and telling her how good she looked, Nay-Nay would turn to me and say: "Hair that long and thick? Give me a break! That's a hairpiece if ever I saw one. . . . Since when have you known her teeth to be that white and straight? I bet she spent a fortune on implants. . . . She's not foolin' me, those are falsies. Notice how she didn't admit that they weren't really hers when I complimented them? I respect women who keep it real—women who're not pretending to be beauty queens, who will let you know they're just 'regular' folks like me and you."

Nay-Nay went on to tell me about one of her "regular" friends who, at the drop of an eyelash would disclose her womanly secrets. According to Nay, no matter where you are or whom you're with, if you compliment this so-called down-to-earth beauty queen, she will quickly assure you that her hair is a weave job, her nails are press-ons, and her boobs are padded.

I looked at Nay-Nay and, for the first time, as it relates to our friendship, I thought of what my mother used to say: "The best mirror is an old friend."

Suddenly, even though I've always put a lot into maintaining my friendships with my women friends, I was convinced that Nay-Nay and I would be better off as acquaintances rather than friends. I don't ever want to become the kind of woman who makes another woman feel that she has to remove her wig, pull out her false teeth, take out her colored contacts, or yank the padding out of her bra to prove to me that there's nothing special about her. My point is if you are the envy-hearted, fault-finding kind, I encourage you to begin planting seeds of improvement in your life. Take an etiquette class or learn to cook ten things better than anybody else can cook them. If you inject positive things in your life, you won't have to go around being hateful and begrudging other women of their time in the sun.

Since we're on the subject of reaping what you sow, harvest time is my favorite time of year because what I've tended all year finally comes back to me. To a pie baker, there's nothing better than fruits rushed from the tree to a waiting pie crust. I love to see what I can create with the best of the season—the delicious apples, juicy peaches, and sweet pears. But I must confess, not all of my seasons produce bumper crops. There are times when the crows swoop in and gobble up every seed, every good thing that I've tried to do for myself. When that happens, I remember what my mother used to say, "You can't let a bad harvest stop you from sowing—after a bad harvest, sow again" and then I'm okay.

Miss Hatfield and Her Jelly Pies

Miss Hatfield lived a few houses away from our house. She was a tall, handsome woman who dressed in tailored suits and enunciated her words by the book, much like an English schoolteacher would. For years, Miss Hatfield lived in a big white house with her sickly mother, Old Lady Hatfield, who was mean and ornery. The elder once yelled admonitions at a group of children because they were leaving a trail of pine needle droppings in front of her house as they dragged a Christmas tree home. Most folks preferred to cross the street than to pass in front of the Hatfield house.

In the summer when the screens were in, the most delectable aromas drifted out of Miss Hatfield's kitchen window and wafted up the street to where we were lounging on the wicker chairs that my mother had salvaged and meticulously repaired. Miss Hatfield kept to herself; she was standoffish, so we didn't know much about her. But my mother used to say, "You can tell a lot about a woman by the way her cooking smells."

When Old Lady Hatfield died, Miss Hatfield started reaching out to the neighborhood. She would smile and wave as she drove by in her sparkling white Buick. Sometimes she honked the horn. She started passing out home-baked goods, like peace offerings. We especially liked her jelly pies.

- One 9-inch single Flaky Pie Crust (page 8), rolled out, fitted into a pie plate, and edge trimmed and crimped
- ½ cup sugar
- ½ cup (1 stick) unsalted butter, softened
- 4 large eggs
- 1 teaspoon vanilla extract
- 1 cup jelly (any flavor)

Makes one 9-inch pie

Preheat the oven to 350 degrees. Prepare the pie crust and set aside.

Cream the sugar and butter together in a medium-size bowl. Separate the egg yolks from the egg whites. Set the egg whites aside. In a separate bowl, beat the yolks until light and fluffy, then add them to the sugar-and-butter mixture and mix thoroughly. Stir in the egg whites, mixing thoroughly. Stir in the vanilla and jelly. Spoon the filling into the pie crust. Place in the oven and bake until the edge of the crust is golden brown, 40 to 45 minutes. Let cool completely on a wire rack before serving.

Apricot Jam Tart

In an era when women are expected to stand on their own two feet, I'm almost too embarrassed to admit that I am still fascinated by a woman like Geneva Hardaway. She was an older woman I met many years ago while I was working as a letter carrier in an aging, lackluster neighborhood.

Miss Geneva, who had to be in her early fifties, was different from most of the stay-at-home-women whom I had known. First of all, she was a stay-at-home woman, not a stay-at-home housewife or a stay-at-home mom; if you didn't know it, I'm here to tell you, there's a real distinction between them. Miss Geneva was soft-spoken and stylish in a womanly kind of way. When you are a young sensitive woman, slopping through rain, sleet, and snow, it's easy to develop a certain sensibility toward any woman who answers her door in the middle of the day wearing satin robes and feathery slippers. For me, especially on an inclement day, a fancy, housebound woman like Miss Geneva was an exotic creature to be observed and studied.

Fortunately, Miss Geneva's beautiful kitchen eventually became a sanctuary for me—a cold glass of water here and there and, now and then, a stirring conversation about womanhood. Through our conversations, I learned that she was the kind of woman men gave money and jewelry to. She loved to show off her jewelry (she kept a lot of it hidden in her enchanted kitchen, in teacups and sugar bowls) and I enjoyed looking at her beautiful pieces. I loved how she handled them—in that tender way women finger the trinkets that men give them—while she was telling her stories. "No matter how important a man is," she once said, "there is a woman out there who he'll spend time with and give his money to. If a man's going to be with me, I've got to be that woman."

Once, when I was going through a stormy phase and wanted to know this sort of thing, I asked Miss Geneva, "How does a woman ask a man for money and things? How do you do it? Did your mother teach you what to say?"

Geneva Hardaway looked at me and in her soft, confidential voice she chuckled. "Sweetie," she said, "I've never had to ask a man for anything. My mother taught me how to dress up and how to cook well. Those two attributes always did the asking, they always spoke for themselves."

Miss Geneva's influence is still with me. If you have the eyes to see it and the ears to hear it, you can experience an empowering sensation, sitting in a woman's warm kitchen, looking at her jewels, and listening to her stories; it's something that you never forget. Sometimes, even now, when it's raining outside and I'm on my way to work, I think of Miss Geneva, and I still wish I knew how to ask a man for money.

I do know that Miss Geneva was a wonderful cook, but I don't know if she ever made apricot tarts or apricot anything for that matter. What compels me to tell her story here is the fact that apricot is such a vibrant, sexy color, and every time I see it, it reminds me of Miss Geneva, of her satin robes and matching, feathery slippers.

- Dough for one 9-inch double Sweet Tart Crust (page 12) to which you've added 1 tablespoon each grated lemon rind and fresh lemon juice
- 1½ cups chunky-style apricot preserves
- ⅛ teaspoon ground nutmeg
- ⅛ teaspoon ground cinnamon
- 1 tablespoon fresh lemon juice
- Confectioners' sugar for garnish

Makes one 9-inch tart

Preheat the oven to 350 degrees.

Butter a 9-inch tart pan. Press two-thirds of the dough into the bottom and ½ inch up the side of the pan. Set the pan and the remaining dough aside.

Combine the preserves, spices, and lemon juice in a medium-size bowl, then spread over the bottom of the crust.

On a lightly floured work surface, roll out the remaining dough ⅛ inch thick and cut it into 1-inch-wide strips. Weave the strips in a lattice pattern over the top of the tart. Using the tines of a fork, seal the ends of the lattice firmly around the sides of the crust. Place in the oven and bake until the crust is light golden brown, about 30 minutes.

Let cool completely on a wire rack before serving with confectioners' sugar sifted over the top.

Mama's Mock Cherry Pie

Mama used to tell me, "Just because a man doesn't say anything, that doesn't mean he isn't watching." She would tell me how she came to this revelation after she'd let her toenails go for a few days without the red polish she'd worn on them since the day she and Daddy got married. She said, during the forty-something years that she'd meticulously painted them fire-engine red to catch Daddy's attention, he never said one word about them. She finally came to the conclusion that her efforts were going unnoticed and that perhaps she should concentrate her feminine wiles somewhere else. No sooner did she stop painting her toenails than Daddy said, "I used to love the way you kept up your feet; they used to look so pretty. Why you lettin' 'em go all of a sudden?"

Mama said the comment bowled her over. Mama said she promptly called Miss Josie, the lady who did her hair for special occasions, and made an appointment for her first professional pedicure.

Daddy may not have acknowledged Mama's red toenails, but he always told her how nice her dinners were, especially when they included her mock cherry pie. Mama used to say, *I'd stop cooking for a man who wasn't considerate enough to compliment my meals every now and again.*

- Dough for one 9-inch double Flaky Pie Crust (page 8)
- 3 cups fresh cranberries, picked over and chopped
- 1 cup dark seeded raisins
- 1½ cups sugar
- 1 tablespoon cornstarch
- ¼ teaspoon salt
- ¾ cup warm water
- ½ teaspoon vanilla extract

Makes one 9-inch pie

Preheat the oven to 350 degrees.

Gather the dough into two balls, one slightly larger than the other. Refrigerate the smaller ball. On a lightly floured work surface, roll out the larger ball into a 12-inch circle, about ⅛ inch thick. Place a 9-inch pie plate upside down on top of it. Use a small knife to cut a 1-inch border around the plate. Remove the plate. Fold one side of the crust over in half. Fold the crust into quarters. Place it so that the center point is positioned in the center of the plate. Unfold the dough and press it firmly into the pie plate. Refrigerate until you need it.

In a large bowl, combine the cranberries, raisins, sugar, cornstarch, and salt and toss until the fruit is well coated. Stir in the water and vanilla. Pour the filling into the pie crust. Remove the dough for the top crust from the refrigerator and roll it out into an 11-inch circle the same way you rolled out the bottom crust. Lay the top crust over the filling. Trim and crimp the edges together with the tines of a fork to seal. Cut slits in the top to allow the steam to escape. Place in the oven and bake until the crust is nice and golden and the juices are bubbly, 45 to 50 minutes. Let cool completely on a wire rack.

My Grandmother's Handmade Apple Pie

My grandmother believed that she could look at a woman's hands and tell whether or not she was a good cook. "Good cooks have good hands," she used to say. According to my grandmother, good cooking hands are hands that are sturdy, but not too heavy; gentle, but not too weak; have good movement, but aren't too prissy.

My grandmother had good cooking hands. They were full of energy and were always doing something—for herself and for others. When they weren't arched in prayer, they were washing dishes or hanging out clothes, taking a pot of soup to a shut-in, or adjusting the brim of a new church hat that she'd just bought. When her hands weren't rubbing Jergens® lotion into her skin, one hand was painting the nails on the other with clear nail polish. My grandmother worked diligently to keep her hands groomed. That was her daily beauty regimen. To me, my grandmother's hands were at their best when they were rolling out pie dough or weaving a lattice top on one of her lovely pies.

My grandmother used to say, "You can bring out the taste better when you use your hands."

Dough for one 9-inch double Flaky Pie Crust (page 8)

8 Golden Delicious apples (or any firm cooking apples), peeled, cored, and thinly sliced

1 tablespoon fresh lemon juice

½ cup granulated sugar

½ cup firmly packed light brown sugar

2½ tablespoons all-purpose flour

¾ teaspoon ground cinnamon

¼ teaspoon ground nutmeg

⅛ teaspoon salt

2 tablespoons unsalted butter, cut into small pieces

1 small egg, beaten together with 1 teaspoon water (optional)

¼ teaspoon each granulated sugar and ground cinnamon mixed together (optional)

Makes one 9-inch pie

Preheat the oven to 375 degrees

Gather the dough into two balls, one slightly larger than the other. Refrigerate the smaller ball of dough. On a lightly floured work surface, roll out the larger ball of dough into a 12-inch circle, about ⅛ inch thick. Place a 9-inch pie plate upside down on top of the rolled-out dough. Using a small knife, cut around the plate, leaving a 1-inch border of dough around the plate. Remove the plate. Fold one side of the crust over in half. Fold the crust into quarters. Pick up the crust so the center point is positioned in the center of the plate. Unfold the dough and press it firmly into the pie plate. Refrigerate the crust until you need it.

Place the apples in a medium-size bowl and sprinkle with the lemon juice, then toss lightly to coat. In another medium-size bowl, combine both sugars, the flour, spices, and salt, and sprinkle this over the apples. Toss the apples until well coated with the mixture. Remove the bottom crust from the refrigerator and pour the apples into it, then dot them with the butter. Remove the dough for the top crust from the refrigerator and roll it out into an 11-inch circle the same way you rolled out the bottom crust. Lay the top crust over the filling. Trim and flute the edges.

Gather together the dough scraps and roll them out on a lightly floured surface. Using a small cookie cutter, cut out small shapes, or press pretty designs into the scraps using the decorative end of an old thread spool that's been sprayed with nonstick cooking spray. If you like, brush the back of each cutout with the egg wash, then lay the cutout on the crust, moistened side down. Cut slits in the top of the pie to allow steam to escape. If you like, sprinkle the cinnamon sugar mixture evenly over the top.

Place the pie in the oven and bake until the filling is bubbly and the crust golden brown, 50 to 60 minutes.

Let cool on a wire rack for about 30 minutes to let the juices settle before serving. Serve warm or at room temperature.

Pink Lady Apple Pie

My grandmother used to say, "Men expect women to be particular. As women, we shouldn't disappoint them." My grandmother had high standards. When she sent my grandfather to market she asked for the sweetest strawberries, the ripest bananas, the juiciest lemons. Her message was, only the best will do.

Not long ago, my friend T.C. asked if I would make his favorite dessert—apple pie. I said, "Sure. But on your way over, I'll need you to stop by the market and pick up a bag of Pink Lady apples." Of course, Golden Delicious would have done just fine. But I was doing what my grandmother would have done—asking for a higher standard.

- Dough for one 9-inch double Flaky Pie Crust (page 8)
- 1 cup sugar, plus ½ teaspoon for sprinkling
- ½ teaspoon freshly grated nutmeg
- ½ teaspoon ground cinnamon
- ⅛ teaspoon ground cloves
- 2 tablespoons all-purpose flour
- ½ teaspoon vanilla extract
- 8 medium-size Pink Lady apples (or any good pie apple), peeled, cored, and sliced
- 1 tablespoon unsalted butter, cut into small pieces
- 1 teaspoon milk (optional)

Makes one 9-inch pie

Preheat the oven to 350 degrees.

Gather the dough into two balls, one slightly larger than the other. Refrigerate the smaller one. On a lightly floured work surface, roll out the larger ball of dough, into 12-inch circle about ⅛ inch thick. Place a 9-inch pie plate upside down on top of the rolled-out dough. Use a small knife to cut a 1-inch border around the pie plate. Remove the plate. Fold one side of the crust over in half. Fold the crust into quarters. Pick up the crust so that the center point is positioned in the center of the plate. Unfold the dough and press it firmly into the pie plate. Refrigerate until you need it.

In a large bowl, combine 1 cup of the sugar, the spices, and flour until well blended. Sprinkle evenly with the vanilla, a few drops at a time. Add the apples and toss until well coated. Remove the bottom crust from the refrigerator. Pour the filling into the pie crust, then dot it with the butter.

Remove the smaller ball of dough from the refrigerator and roll it out into an 11-inch circle the same way you did the bottom crust. Lay the top crust over the filling. Trim the overhang to ½ inch. Fold the edge of the top crust under the edge of the bottom crust until the edges are even with the rim of the pie plate. Flute all around the edge with your fingers. Cut steam vents in the top crust. If you like, brush the crust with the milk, then sprinkle it with the remaining ½ teaspoon sugar.

Place in the oven and bake until bubbly and golden, about 1 hour. Let cool completely on a wire rack before serving with vanilla ice cream, or a wedge of cheddar cheese.

Aunt Helen's Pineapple Pie

Months before I got married, I purchased a thick notebook and drove thirty miles every Saturday morning to my Aunt Helen's house in Flint, Michigan, where I would sit at her kitchen table and copy down her recipes and cooking secrets. Cooking for a man was Aunt Helen's specialty; her cupboards were stocked with seasonings like rosemary, basil, and sage and spices like cardamom, nutmeg, and anise seed. I wanted to know what she put in her collard greens to give them their sweet, tender nature; what she did to get that delicious, crunchy crust at the bottom of her cornbread. I wanted to know why her pound cakes were moister than anybody else's, and why her pie crusts were always so flavorful and flaky. In essence, I wanted to learn how to cook so that my cooking would bring my husband home every night in time for supper. Aunt Helen, who delights in the spotlight cast upon her culinary skills, had the patience of Job.

Because my late Aunt Bessie's pineapple pie recipe—included in my dessert cookbook *Sweets*—stirred up wonderful reviews, including that by the food writer Kate Lawson of *The Detroit News*, who said the pie was lip-smacking delicious, Aunt Helen, who's not one to be outdone in the kitchen, wanted me to give you her mouthwatering version of this family treat. And you can believe, if Aunt Helen puts her stamp of approval on a recipe, you're in for a treat.

- One 9-inch single Flaky Pie Crust (page 8), rolled out, fitted into a pie plate, and edge trimmed and crimped
- 3 large eggs
- 1 cup sugar
- 1 tablespoon all-purpose flour
- ¼ cup light corn syrup
- ¼ cup (½ stick) unsalted butter, melted
- 1 cup canned crushed pineapple, drained
- 1 teaspoon vanilla extract

Makes one 9-inch pie

Preheat the oven to 350 degrees. Prepare the pie crust and set aside.

Crack the eggs over a large bowl and beat with an electric mixer on medium speed until light and fluffy. Add the sugar, flour, corn syrup, and melted butter and thoroughly combine using a big mixing spoon. Add the crushed pineapple and vanilla and gently stir until well blended. Pour the filling into the crust. Place in the oven and bake until the crust is nice and golden and the filling is set in the center, about 45 minutes. I prefer to serve this pie plain and at room temperature.

Mamie Short's Lemon Sponge Pie

Miss Mamie lives across the street in a gorgeous brick house. For as long as I've known her, she's driven BMWs and Cadillacs, and worn marabou slippers and gorgeous designer housedresses out to the mailbox at the end of her long driveway. On the weekends when I am home and indulging in the womanish things that replenish my soul, I enjoy looking out the window at Miss Mamie promenading down her winding driveway to her mailbox or strolling around her perfect lawn, stopping here and there to baby one of her beautiful potted plants.

Watching Miss Mamie sauntering around her yard in her silks and satins reminds me that dressing up in sexy, luscious fabrics and feminine adornments shouldn't be limited to special evenings and vacations. It's such a wonderful thing to be alive and feminine, and to want to dress up and show it from time to time—even if the only place that you're going is to the mailbox at the end of your driveway.

- One 9-inch single Flaky Pie Crust (page 8), rolled out, fitted into a pie plate, and edge trimmed and crimped
- ¼ cup (½ stick) unsalted butter, softened
- 1 cup plus 2 tablespoons sugar
- 3 large eggs, separated
- 3 tablespoons all-purpose flour
- ⅛ teaspoon salt
- 1½ cups whole milk
- Grated rind and juice of 1 lemon

Makes one 9-inch pie

Preheat the oven to 350 degrees. Prepare the pie crust and set aside.

In a large bowl, cream together the butter and 1 cup of the sugar until light and fluffy. Beat in the egg yolks, flour, salt, milk, and lemon rind and juice until smooth.

In another large bowl, beat the egg whites with an electric mixer until foamy. Add the remaining 2 tablespoons sugar slowly, beating until soft peaks form. Fold the beaten egg whites into the egg yolk mixture until no streaks of white remain. Pour the filling into the crust. Place in the oven and bake until the top is golden and springs back when lightly touched, 30 to 35 minutes. Be careful not to overbake. Let cool completely on a wire rack before serving. Miss Mamie says she refrigerates her pie for an hour or so before serving. Garnish with a dollop of whipped cream.

Aunt Betty Jean's Lemon Pie

When I was a little girl, my Aunt Betty Jean was a teenager. Aunt Betty had lots of clothes, lots of jewelry, lots of records, and a red convertible car. I loved to sit in the back seat of her convertible as we zipped around our small town. I would throw my head back and poke out my chest; I felt like a movie star. All these years later, I still remember how the wind brushed over my face and how exhilarated I felt.

Aunt Betty says she doesn't recall it now, but I remember going with her to one of her girlfriend's houses. The girl was young, married, and had a baby. Her house was stuffy, in disarray, and all she talked about were bills, changing diapers, not having a car, and cheating husbands. She kept telling Aunt Betty, "Girl, you've got it made." What I remember most about the visit was how sad I felt for the girl and how relieved I was to leave. I remember looking at my aunt through the rear view mirror, seeing the wind blowing through her hair, and thinking, Girl, you really do have it made.

Eventually, Aunt Betty got married and made her own life. Over the years, she's developed such a natural flair for taking lemons and fashioning them into something so divine, that now, whenever we gather, we count on her to bring something lemony that we can pass around the table.

- One 9-inch single Flaky Pie Crust (page 8), rolled out, fitted into a pie plate, and edge trimmed and crimped
- 1 cup sugar
- 1 tablespoon all-purpose flour
- 4 large eggs, beaten
- 1 cup light corn syrup
- ¼ cup (½ stick) unsalted butter, melted
- 1 tablespoon grated lemon rind
- ¼ cup fresh lemon juice
- Whipped cream and thinly sliced lemon rinds for garnishing

Makes one 9-inch pie

Preheat the oven to 350 degrees. Prepare the pie crust and set aside.

In a medium-size bowl, combine the sugar and flour, then add the eggs and corn syrup, mixing well. Stir in the melted butter and lemon rind and juice. Pour the filling into the crust, place in the oven, and bake until the crust is golden, 45 to 50 minutes. Let cool completely on a wire rack.

Garnish each serving with a dollop of fresh whipped cream and a thin twist of lemon rind.

Miss Maude McCracken's Rhubarb Pie

When I was about ten, I saw a red coat on a little-girl mannequin in a downtown department store window. Even then, I understood the allure of the color red on a woman. I said to my mother, "I sure would like to have that coat." My mother said, "You can have just about anything in this world that you want to have, if you put your mind to it." I knew what that meant. Mama wasn't going to just give me the money for the coat; she was always trying to raise me to a higher level of thinking. If I wanted the little red coat in the window, I would have to earn it.

Maude McCracken was the kind of old lady who wore wool coats with fox tails and fox heads attached to them; she had a matching hat for every coat. People used to say, "That Maude McCracken sure knows a fine coat when she sees one; her coats have the most wonderful fur collars." When I was a little, little girl, I didn't like Miss McCracken's coats. When we saw her at the meat market or stood next to her in line at the bank, I believed the beady eyes of the animals on her coats were glaring at me. I imagined that the critters were poised to leap off her chest and onto mine at any moment. When we went to visit Miss McCracken—her and my great aunt, Big Mama, were good friends—Miss McCracken dominated the conversations with various versions of "I could have really been somebody if only . . ." But my attention wasn't on conversations or the plate of goodies she always set before us; the whole time we were there, I kept my legs elevated and my eyes glued to the floor. In my little mind, it was plausible that one of her coat critters could come running through the room at any moment.

Shortly after I spotted that gorgeous little red number in the department store window, my great aunt sent me to Miss Maude's house on an errand. Miss Maude had fixed a couple

of rhubarb pies—one for herself and one for Big Mama. For once, I was happy to go to Miss Maude's house. I knew that if anybody understood how bad I wanted that little red coat, how owning it would make me feel like somebody, it would be Maude McCracken.

I stood in Miss McCracken's kitchen that day, as grown as any little woman, and told her about the little coat and how badly I wanted it. "I need to earn some money," I said. "I could water your plants, dust your furniture, and sweep your kitchen floor." Miss McCracken looked at me with the compassion that people who love the same thing have for one another. "Well," said Miss McCracken, "I've got a heap of rhubarb from my garden that I'm trying to get rid of. I thought I'd send a box of pies to the Civitan Center. I reckon I could use some help."

And that's how I came to own my first red coat—a divine understanding between two coat lovers. With the money I earned, peeling and mixing and stirring, I was able to put a nice down-payment on the coat. In those days, you could lay away just about anything.

My mother seemed to get a kick out of taking me to the department store and watching me pay on my account. The first time Miss McCracken saw me in my little red coat, she said, "Gracious, Lord, that's one fine coat." Coming from Miss McCracken, a woman who knew a fine coat when she saw one, that was the ultimate compliment.

- One 9-inch single Flaky Pie Crust (page 8), rolled out, fitted into a pie plate, and edge trimmed and crimped
- 1¼ cups sugar
- ¼ cup all-purpose flour
- ¼ teaspoon ground cloves
- ½ teaspoon grated orange rind
- ¼ cup orange juice
- 2 tablespoons unsalted butter, cut into small pieces
- 4 cups trimmed red rhubarb stalks, sliced 1 inch thick

CRUMB TOPPING

- 1 cup all-purpose flour
- ¼ teaspoon salt
- ½ cup sugar
- ¼ cup (½ stick) unsalted butter, softened

Makes one 9-inch pie

Preheat the oven to 425 degrees. Prepare the pie crust and set aside.

Combine the sugar, flour, and cloves in a medium-size, heavy saucepan and whisk until well blended. Stir in the orange rind and juice, and the butter. Cook over low to medium heat, stirring, until thickened and bubbly, then add the rhubarb. Stir to coat the rhubarb, then remove from the heat and spoon the filling into the crust. Place in the oven and bake until the rhubarb is tender and the juice bubbles, about 30 minutes.

Meanwhile, make the crumb topping. In a small bowl, whisk together the flour, salt, and sugar. Add the butter and, using your fingertips, work it into the dry mixture until pea-sized crumbs form.

Take the pie out of the oven and sprinkle evenly with the topping. Return to the oven and bake until the topping is golden brown, 10 to 15 minutes longer. Let cool on a wire rack for at least 15 minutes before serving.

Miss Mattie Clyde Parker's Frozen Citrus Pie

In an era where instant messaging and emails seem to be the order, talk nowadays is effortless, becoming cheap. That's why I hope true benevolence between women never goes away. Because sometimes you may be going through something for which you need more than just cheap talk; considerable or small, sometimes you need a little action to go along with the talk—somebody to come by and sit with you for a spell, or to send something by that says, "I may not know exactly what you're going through, but . . . . "

Miss Mattie Clyde is a sweet lady who does all kinds of sweet things for the church and our community. Out of all of her considerate acts, my favorite is when she brings one of her luscious pies to pass. I especially like her frozen citrus pies.

Compassion may be hard to find, but we always know it when we taste it.

- 1¼ cups graham cracker crumbs (about 18 graham cracker squares crushed fine)
- ¼ cup sugar
- ¼ cup (½ stick) unsalted butter, melted
- One 8-ounce container whipped vanilla dessert topping (such as Cool Whip)
- One 14-ounce can sweetened condensed milk, chilled
- One 6-ounce can frozen citrus concentrate (any flavor), thawed
- Few drops of corresponding food coloring (optional)
- 1 thin, sugar-coated slice of citrus for garnish (optional)

Makes one 9-inch pie

In a medium-size bowl, mix together the crumbs, sugar, and melted butter until the crumbs have absorbed the butter. Pour the crumbs into a 9-inch pie plate and firmly pat them into the bottom and up the sides of the plate, creating a compact and uniform crust. Place in the freezer and chill for at least 30 minutes.

In another medium-size bowl, combine the dessert topping, condensed milk, and thawed concentrate. If you want to, stir in a few drops of food coloring, such as yellow for lemonade. Thoroughly blend the ingredients, so the filling is smooth and creamy, not runny.

Pour the filling into the crust. Use a spatula to level the filling even with the rim of the crust. If desired, garnish with a the slice of citrus. Cover with plastic wrap and freeze for several hours or overnight.

Let the pie stand at room temperature for 10 minutes to make slicing easier.

Cousin Gwendolyn's Deep-Dish Mandarin Orange Pie

My lovely cousin Gwendolyn Morgan once told me that the message a woman's appearance and presentation in the kitchen sends out is just as significant as it is in other parts of the house. To that end, Cousin Gwen has a stunning wardrobe of flowing housedresses and silky pajama sets that move gracefully from one room in her house to the other.

Gwendolyn is no stranger to being in the presence of men who know their way around a kitchen. Gwen's father, Cousin Willie Gill, owned and operated Gill's Bakery in Kalamazoo, Michigan, where his handmade cakes, pies, and donuts were as flavorsome as any woman's. Gwen is married to Ed, who is an excellent cook. Gwen says, because of Ed's flexible schedule—he's home from work before she is—he has taken the lead in cooking. According to Cousin Gwen, there aren't many things more fulfilling than living with a man who can find his way from the pantry to the stove. Still, every now and then, she feels compelled to slip into one of her graceful housedresses and cook Ed a little something sweet, with just a touch of vamp in it.

According to Cousin Gwen, there aren't many things more fulfilling than living with a man who can find his way from the pantry to the stove.

Dough for one 9-inch double deep-dish Flaky Pie Crust (page 8)

Two 8.4-ounce cans (3 cups) Mandarin orange segments

½ cup sugar, plus ½ teaspoon for sprinkling

3 tablespoons all-purpose flour

½ teaspoon ground nutmeg

⅛ teaspoon salt

½ teaspoon vanilla extract

¼ teaspoon orange extract

2 tablespoons unsalted butter

1 teaspoon milk (optional)

Makes one 9-inch deep-dish pie

Preheat the oven to 350 degrees.

Divide the dough into two balls, one slightly larger than the other. Refrigerate the smaller ball. On a lightly floured work surface, roll out the larger ball of dough into a 12-inch circle, about ⅛ inch thick. Place a 9-inch deep-dish pie plate upside down on top of the rolled out dough. Using a small knife, cut around the plate, leaving a 1-inch border of dough around the plate. Remove the plate. Fold one side of the crust over in half. Fold the crust into quarters. Pick up the crust so the center point is positioned in the center of the plate. Unfold the dough and press it firmly into the pie plate. Refrigerate the crust until you need it.

Open the cans of oranges. Drain the syrup from each can into a medium-size container. Set the orange segments to the side. Measure 1 cup of the syrup into a medium-size saucepan. Sift 1 cup of the sugar, the flour, nutmeg, and salt into a small bowl, then pour the mixture into the saucepan. Over low heat, whisk the mixture until smooth and lump free. Stir in the extracts and continue stirring until well mixed and the syrup has thickened. Add the butter and stir until melted. Gently fold in the oranges and remove from the heat. Remove the bottom crust from the refrigerator and pour the syrupy oranges into it.

Remove the dough for the top crust from the refrigerator and roll out into an 11-inch circle the same way you did the bottom crust. Lay the top crust over the filling. Trim the overhang to ½ inch. Fold the edge of the top crust under the edge of the bottom crust until the edges are even with the rim of the pie plate. Flute all around the crust with your fingers. If you wish, brush the top with a little milk, sprinkle on a little sugar, then cut a couple of steam holes in the top.

Place in the oven and bake until it turns brown and bubbly, 40 to 45 minutes. Let cool on a wire rack for about 30 minutes.

Serve this up with a dollop of whipped topping or vanilla ice cream.

Sister Curry's Orange Tang® Pie

CRUST

- 1¼ cups all-purpose flour
- One 3-ounce box instant vanilla pudding mix
- 1 cup chopped pecans
- ½ cup (1 stick) cold unsalted butter, cubed
- 1 large egg, beaten

FILLING

- One 8-ounce carton sour cream
- One 14-ounce can sweetened condensed milk
- ½ cup Tang orange drink mix
- ⅛ teaspoon salt
- ¼ teaspoon orange extract
- One 12-ounce container whipped dessert topping (such as Cool Whip)
- Thinly sliced orange slices for garnish (optional)

Makes one 9 x 13-inch pie

I just adore Sister Curry. It was friendship at first sight. She's so sweet; she's always got a smile on her face—even while she's talking to you, she's smiling and calling you "Love." Sister Curry, who recognizes that from time to time I can get a little stuck on the trivial stuff if I'm not careful, always reminds me, "You've got to learn to eat the meat, and spit out the bones, Love."

Sister Curry says she couldn't tell you exactly what it is that makes people weak in the knees when they eat her orange Tang pie. She imagines a lot of the pie's allure has to do with its sweet orange flavor and mild orange aroma.

Preheat the oven to 350 degrees. Grease a 9 x 13-inch baking dish and set aside.

Combine the flour, pudding mix, and pecans in a large bowl. Work the butter cubes into the mixture, using a fork or your fingers, until it resembles garden peas. Add the egg and mix until well combined. Spread the crust evenly over the bottom of the baking dish, patting it down. Bake until lightly browned, 10 to 15 minutes. Don't let it get overly brown. Set aside to cool.

Combine the sour cream and condensed milk in a large bowl. Stir in the orange drink mix, then the salt and orange extract. Gently fold in the dessert topping until the mixture is thick and fluffy. Spread the filling over the cooled pie crust. Cover with plastic wrap and place in the refrigerator until set, 2 to 3 hours.

Sister Curry garnishes the top of her pie with twists of thinly sliced oranges.

Benita's Any Flavor Cobbler

When we were teenagers, my friend Benita used to say, "When I have a husband I'm gonna get up every morning before he does—brush my teeth, wash my face, curl my hair, put red lipstick on, put false eyelashes on, spritz myself with perfume, and then get back into bed. So when he wakes up he will think, my wife is something else."

When I am in the company of Benita and her husband, Fidel, Benita proudly tells me that over the course of her twenty-year marriage, she has been a dutiful wife and that, like she said all those years ago, Fidel has never seen her without her hair and face nicely done. While she confesses that it hasn't always been easy, getting up an hour earlier than she's had to (and judging from the drained look on her face, I believe her) in order to present herself fresh and beautiful at sunrise, she says with a smile, it's been well worth it. On this particular day, Benita glances lovingly at her husband who is sitting at the kitchen table reading *The Free Press*. "Fidel appreciates having a wife who keeps after her appearance; don't 'choo, baby?"

When I glance over at Fidel, he appears unmoved by his wife's exhausting efforts to keep herself looking beautiful for him. In fact, the only thing Fidel seems concerned with is the cobbler that's cooking in the oven. *"Que pasa?"* he asks. "Why isn't it done yet?"

½ cup (1 stick) unsalted butter
1 cup all-purpose flour
1 cup sugar
1 teaspoon baking powder
1 cup milk
1 teaspoon vanilla extract
One 20-ounce can pie filling, any flavor

Makes one 9 x 13-inch cobbler

In an oven set at 250 degrees, melt the butter in a 9 x 13-inch baking dish.

Mix the flour, sugar, baking powder together in a medium-size bowl. Add the milk and vanilla and stir until the mixture forms a smooth batter. Remove the dish from the oven when the butter has melted. Pour the batter evenly over the melted butter. Do not stir. Gently pour the can of pie filling along the middle of the batter. Do not stir. Increase the oven temperature to 350 degrees and wait 10 minutes before placing the cobbler in the oven. Bake until golden brown, about 30 minutes. Let cool on a wire rack for about 30 minutes, then serve it still warm, with vanilla ice cream or whipped cream—at least, that's how I like it.

Mayor Ham's Brown Sugar Peach Pie

Somebody once said, you are what you say, and, if that's true, it explains why our illustrious mayor, Miss Wilmer Ham, is such a wonderful dessert cook. Wherever you see her, she greets you with a sugary salutation, "How you doin', Sugar Plum?

The civic motto of our mayor, "I don't promise what I can't deliver," is the same one she uses in life and in the kitchen. Nothing smells or tastes as good as Miss Ham's brown sugar peach pie.

- Dough for one 9-inch double Flaky Pie Crust (page 8)
- ¾ cup firmly packed dark brown sugar
- 3 tablespoons all-purpose flour
- 3 tablespoons light corn syrup
- 2 tablespoons unsalted butter, softened
- ½ teaspoon ground cinnamon
- ½ teaspoon ground nutmeg
- ⅛ teaspoon ground cloves
- 5 cups peeled, pitted, and sliced ripe peaches
- 1 tablespoon fresh lemon juice

Makes one 9-inch pie

Preheat the oven to 425 degrees.

Divide the dough into two balls, one slightly larger than the other. Refrigerate the smaller ball. On a lightly floured work surface, roll out the larger ball of dough into a 12-inch circle, about ⅛ inch thick. Place a 9-inch pie plate upside down on top of the rolled out dough. Using a small knife, cut around the plate, leaving a 1-inch border of dough around the plate. Remove the plate. Fold one side of the crust over in half. Fold the crust into quarters. Pick up the crust so the center point is positioned in the center of the plate. Unfold the dough and press it firmly into the pie plate. Refrigerate the crust until you need it.

In a medium-size, heavy saucepan, thoroughly combine the brown sugar and flour. Stir in the corn syrup, butter, and spices. Cook over low heat, stirring constantly, until the sugar is dissolved. Arrange the peaches over the crust, then sprinkle them with the lemon juice. Pour the brown sugar mixture evenly over the peaches.

Remove the dough for the top crust from the refrigerator and roll out into an 11-inch circle the same way you did the bottom crust. Cut the crust into strips that are about ½ inch wide. Lay half the strips in one direction, so they are positioned from the top to the bottom of the pie pan (from 12 o'clock to 6 o'clock). Lay the remaining strips directly on top of the first strips, so they are going from side to side (from 9 o'clock to 3 o'clock). Trim the ends of the strips so they are even with the edge of the dough. Crimp all around the edge of the pie.

Place the pie on the lowest rack in the oven and bake until the filling bubbles and the crust is golden brown, 35 to 45 minutes. Let cool for about 20 minutes on a wire rack before serving each portion warm with a scoop of vanilla ice cream.

Miss Oleda Halliburton's Easy Pear Pie on a Baking Sheet

When I was younger, Mama had a friend named Miss Oleda, who seemed to be stuck in a state of anxiety. The woman worried about everything, especially about things having to do with her smiley, broad-shouldered husband, Cecil.

Whenever Mama asked Miss Oleda about Cecil, Miss Oleda would sigh and say, "He's a man and I don't trust him no farther than I can see him."

I once made a comment about Miss Oleda's anxieties, something like, "A woman that nice looking shouldn't be so anxious about a man," to which Mama replied, "Honey, it don't matter who you are or how you look, when you've got a man, you've got something to worry about."

Miss Oleda may have lacked assurance when it came to her husband's commitment to their relationship, but when she brought over one of her delicious pear pies to sample, it was evident where her confidence lay; it was locked inside her cooking.

- Dough for one 9-inch single Flaky Pie Crust (page 8)
- 1 cup sugar (a little more or a little less, depending on the sweetness of the pears), plus 1 teaspoon for sprinkling
- 2 tablespoons cornstarch
- 1 tablespoon ground cinnamon
- 5 cups peeled, cored, and thinly sliced firm pears
- 2 teaspoons vanilla extract
- 1 large egg white, lightly beaten

Makes one 12-inch pie

Preheat the oven to 350 degrees.

On a lightly floured work surface, roll out the crust to a 1/8-inch-thick, 16-inch circle. Transfer it to an aluminum foil–lined baking sheet, making sure to press out any creases; set aside.

In a good-sized bowl, combine 1 cup of the sugar (add more, or less, to suit your taste), the cornstarch, and cinnamon. Add the pears and vanilla, and, using a large fork, toss to coat with the mixture. Spoon the pears into the center of the crust, spreading them to within 2 inches of the edge. Bring the crust up over the pears to form a border of about 2 inches, pleating and folding the crust as needed. To give the pie a polished look, brush the folded edge with the lightly beaten egg white and sprinkle with the remaining 1 teaspoon sugar. Place in the oven and bake until the pears are tender and the crust is a pretty brown, about 20 minutes. Let cool slightly on a wire rack before serving.

6

Nut & Sweet Vegetable Pies

Like most mothers, my mother wanted nothing but the best for her daughter—at work, during play, and in relationships—especially in relationships. Mama used to say, "You can look in a woman's face and tell if she's being treated good at home, 'cause a pleased woman carries a certain sparkle, a certain glow." Mama would go on to tell the story about a relative—a cousin named Edith—who "came home" every year, skinning and grinning, and dripping in furs and diamonds. Mama said Edith was always sitting around boasting about her husband, Lincoln, and how, "Linc gave me this, and Linc gave me that." But Mama said Edith wasn't fooling anybody, leastwise the women in our family. Said, when they'd gather around the table, listening to Edith's tales, they could see in her sinking eyes and washed-out complexion that, in truth, what Lincoln was really giving Edith was the blues.

Mama was a true "rules" girl. "Let him do most of the calling. . . . Sometimes, you have to put him out and shut the door." She was always wary of a man's true intentions; I don't know where that came from, because Daddy was so good to her. She was always reminding me to look deeper, to love with my mind, not just my heart. She was always looking in my face, quietly probing, looking for any sign of trouble. If I told her about some wonderful man that I'd met, she would say, "I know he says he doesn't have anybody, but you be careful; take it slow. 'Cause sometimes a man isn't even aware of how deeply he's been touched by a woman. He may believe he doesn't have another woman, he may call himself through with her; but she could be so deeply embedded inside him, he could never completely leave her even though he might really want to." Mama, who loved the gossip in women's magazines, would add, "If you don't believe me, look at Aristotle Onassis and Maria Callas; at Richard Burton and Elizabeth Taylor."

Mama didn't want to see me get hurt. In fact, even on her deathbed, her last few words to me were of that nature. She said, "Don't run through my money and don't let any man make a fool out of you." Mama believed so passionately in what she was saying, she put emphasis on each word, even though, by then, she was quite frail.

Despite the fact that Mama had rules, she could be very sweet and loyal. Her men friends—her renters, Mr. Youngblood and Mr. Mercer, and Maurice, the man who washed our car—would attest to that; they were always stopping by the house and baring their souls to her. Mr. Youngblood, who had a huge vegetable garden in the country, and a few nut trees growing on a plot of land that he owned, often brought bushels of this or that to the house; he'd marvel the next time he came by and saw the wonderful things—the preserves, relishes, the vegetable and nut pies, and cobblers—that Mama had made from his gifts. Every time I saw Mr. Youngblood, he was dressed up in a suit, replete with a vest, pocket watch, and derby hat. He always smelled spicy, like Old English. He looked a lot like W.C. Fields, except W.C. Fields was white, and Mr. Youngblood, who always had a fat Swisher Sweets® cigar clenched between his tobacco-stained teeth, was as black as the patent leather shoes that he wore.

Whether he had brought Mama her rent money or a food gift, after he'd leave, she'd always say she felt sorry for him; she said he was the kind of man a conniving woman could easily take advantage of—he had a big heart and he was uneducated.

Mama may have been unapproachable with unfamiliar men, but sometimes she would say, "All men are not the same. Not all of them are bad."

Like Mama, I like to do special things with the gifts that people give me, especially the food gifts—jellies and jams, nuts and vegetables. It stirs me when I see expressions of pleasure on people's faces while they're savoring something that's come from my stove-top or out of my oven. As a result, I strive to set a nice table.

I am a firm believer that if you want to turn out a good supper, you have to engage all of your senses in the process of cooking it. I've noticed, when a meal really turns out for me, it's because I've engaged all of my senses—my eyes, my ears, my sense of smell, my hands, and my taste buds—in the cooking process. My grandmother's compliment for that kind of supper was, "Chile, you put your foot in that."

Sherry's Chocolate Chip Pecan Pie

My friend Sherry Draine is a true renaissance woman. Sherry, who recently turned fifty, celebrated her birthday with a series of mini womanish proclamations. For instance, she entered the beauty pageant that *More* magazine holds every year, she took up ballroom dancing, she went to the finest boutique in town and bought herself a lovely beaded gown and matching shoes, then she went downtown and posed regally before a professional portrait artist.

However, while Sherry is truly a modern woman who happily embraces the new understanding and appreciation that we women now have for and about ourselves, she hasn't completely turned away from a lot of the old-fashioned feminine notions that inspired the tipped hats and the chairs being pulled back for our mothers and grandmothers.

Sherry told me about a lingerie event she recently attended. According to Sherry, no sooner had she arrived, the young girls—in their early twenties—hosting the event started grating on her nerves. She said one of the girls would hold up a lacy nightgown or a pair of rhinestone slippers and then, after the more mature women in the audience would blush and giggle—the way we women sometimes do—the young girl would say, "Now, you older women just don't understand; this is the kind of stuff that men like to see." As Sherry told it, this went on for

a while—this *you older women just don't understand* stuff. But the comment that sent Sherry over the top was when one of the girls held up a red nightgown and a bottle of fire-engine red nail polish and said, "I bet you older women don't know how much the color red excites men. . . . especially when they see it on a woman's toes." (Today's "Victoria's Secret" generation can't really believe it invented the rules of womanish seduction, can it?)

Sherry along with the other "older women" in attendance says her time for redemption came when the young girls led the group to their dismal little buffet. Sherry, who's known around town for hosting the loveliest gatherings, said the tablescape lacked character (she has an eye for that sort of thing) and the food was atrocious. According to Sherry, who normally doesn't rub people's faces in their mess, "When the main little girl who was doing all of that *what you older women don't understand* talking cut me a slice of her scorched chocolate pie, I just had to say, 'Darling, you may know what a man likes to see, but I know what a man likes to taste. Remind me to jot down my recipe for chocolate pie; yours is a tad bit off.' "

- One 9-inch single Flaky Pie Crust (page 8), rolled out, fitted into a pie plate, and edge trimmed and crimped
- ½ cup sugar
- ¼ cup (½ stick) unsalted butter, melted
- 3 large eggs, lightly beaten
- 1 cup light corn syrup
- ⅛ teaspoon salt
- 1 teaspoon vanilla extract
- 1½ cups chopped pecans
- 1 cup semisweet chocolate chips

Makes one 9-inch pie

Preheat the oven to 350 degrees. Prepare the pie crust and set aside.

In a medium-size bowl, cream together the sugar and the melted butter until light and creamy. Beat in the eggs. Add the corn syrup, salt, and vanilla and blend until well combined.

Spread the chopped pecans and the chocolate chips evenly over the bottom of the crust, then pour the filling on top. Place in the oven and bake until a knife inserted in the center comes out clean, 50 to 60 minutes. Let cool completely on a wire rack before serving.

The Postmistress's Pecan Cobbler

We've known for a long time that Miss Jacquelyn Vican, the postmistress of our little town, was a hat lady. In fact, over the years I've seen Jacquelyn wear the loveliest hats—from showy lampshade styles to the small and sassy varieties, trimmed in the softest embellishments. In the male-dominated business of letters, Miss Jacquelyn offers no introductions or explanations for her hats; she wears them to work and to business and civic events as though wearing hats should be a way of life.

We may have known that our darling Jacquelyn was a hat lady, but for many it came as a wonderful surprise to discover that she is also a pie lady. It's not uncommon to walk past Jacque's office and see dishes and flatware, and a lovely homemade pie perched on her wooden meeting table. Whenever I pass Miss Jacque's office and see her coifed, yet perfectly engaged in a manly looking business meeting with one of her delicious-looking pie-scapes set to the side, it reminds me that we might live in a man's world, but it wouldn't be worth living in without the wonderful little touches women give it.

1½ cups sugar
¾ cup light corn syrup
¼ cup (½ stick) unsalted butter, melted
½ teaspoon salt
1 tablespoon vanilla extract
6 large eggs, lightly beaten
3 cups coarsely chopped pecans
Dough for one 9-inch double Flaky Pie Crust (page 8)

Makes one 9 x 13-inch cobbler

Preheat the oven to 350 degrees. Grease the inside of a 9 x 13-inch baking dish with cooking oil.

In a large bowl, thoroughly combine the sugar, corn syrup, melted butter, salt, and vanilla. Beat in the eggs. Spread one-third of the mixture over the bottom of the baking dish. Stir the chopped nuts into the remaining mixture and set aside.

On a lightly floured work surface, roll out the dough into a 9 x 13-inch rectangle. Place the rectangle on top of the filling. Spread the remaining nut mixture on top of the crust. Put the cobbler in the oven and bake until the center is almost set, about 50 minutes. Let cool on a wire rack for about 20 minutes, then serve warm or at room temperature with a scoop of vanilla ice cream.

Alberta Beasley's Decadent Pecan Pie

Some working women have a knack for staying feminine. I'm not talking about secretaries and shampoo girls, or bank tellers and schoolteachers. I'm talking about real working women—like traffic cops and construction workers, letter carriers and factory workers—with the kind of jobs that would cause most women to go around looking beat down and cursing like a sailor.

Miss Alberta Beasley was a working woman whose feminine nature was so strong, not even her assembly line job at the car factory could suppress it. In an occupation where brawn and grime and coarse language are the norm, Miss Alberta stood out like a tube of red lipstick in an auto mechanic's tool box.

Miss Alberta, who worked on the line alongside my father, was the apple of my daddy's eye. She was nearly twenty years older than my dad, but he couldn't say enough good things about her. He was always telling my mother how sweet Miss Alberta was and how classy she was; how the perfume that she wore didn't make him sneezy, the way most perfumes did. When Miss Alberta went on her weekend jaunts to Chicago and Baltimore, my daddy told my mother about that, too. Like I said, Miss Alberta had a hold on my daddy.

Mama, who was a lifetime student of the art of womanhood, enjoyed the company of older women. In fact, she used to tell me, *Man has dog, but an old woman who'll share her tricks, now that's a woman's best friend.* Eventually, Mama asked Daddy for an introduction. "I'd like to meet your Miss Alberta," she said.

I won't say that my mother and Alberta Beasley became best friends. They talked on the phone occasionally, occasionally Miss Alberta invited Mama and Daddy over for cards and drinks, and once in a while, she and Mama called upon each other for an exchange of recipes. But Mama never allowed herself to get too intimate with Miss Beasley, not like she did with her other older friend, Miss Ruthie. I guess there was something there that just wouldn't allow it. For one thing, Mama never lost sight of the fact that because Alberta Beasley and Daddy worked side by side, Miss Beasley was as much Daddy's friend as she was Mama's. Just like my grandmother, my mother used to say, "You can't serve two masters and stay true to them both." Mama was young, but she wasn't foolish. After all, Miss Beasley may have been old enough to be Daddy's mother, but she was still a woman—and a sexy, older woman that Daddy thought the world of, at that. According to my grandmother, Miss Beasley was the worst kind of woman—a woman who has full access to your man during his shining moments, his working hours, the time of day when he's putting out his best.

Basically, this is Miss Beasley's recipe; she sent it home by way of Daddy, on a 3 x 5 card, after he carried on over the pecan pie that she brought to an assembly line potluck. But, of course, Mama, who wasn't going to be outdone, took the recipe and put her own stamp on it. Whenever she made it, she'd set aside enough pecans (about 40) to spread on top of the pie to give it that down-home, decadent look, something I doubt Miss Beasley had the mind to do.

- One 9-inch single Flaky Pie Crust (page 8), rolled out, fitted into a pie plate, and edge trimmed and crimped
- 3 large eggs
- 1 cup firmly packed dark brown sugar
- 1 cup light corn syrup, plus more for drizzling
- ¼ cup (½ stick) unsalted butter, melted
- 1 tablespoon all-purpose flour
- 1 teaspoon vanilla extract
- ⅛ teaspoon salt
- 1½ cups chopped pecans
- Enough pecan halves to garnish the top of the pie (optional)

Makes one 9-inch pie

Preheat the oven to 425 degrees. Prepare the pie crust and set aside.

In a medium-size bowl, gently beat the eggs with a whisk or a fork until frothy. Stir in the brown sugar, corn syrup, and melted butter then blend in the flour. Stir in the vanilla and salt. Fold in the chopped pecans. Pour the filling into the pie crust. Arrange the pecan halves on top so the pie looks tempting: just picture in your mind the most delicious-looking pecan pie you've ever seen. At this point, Mama would drizzle a thin line of corn syrup on top of the pecan halves.

Place in the oven and bake for 15 minutes, then reduce the oven temperature to 350 degrees. Continue to bake for another 30 minutes. Watch closely, because you don't want to overcook it and end up with a hard, dry pie. When the pie is done, the edges will be set, but there will be a little wiggle in the center. Let cool completely on a wire rack before serving.

Walnut-Raisin Pie from Elizabethtown

In the early 1970s, I accompanied my mother and father on a long road trip that meandered along the back roads of several southern states. Mama, who had a name for everything, called it our "Bohemian Adventure." To prove her point, she said, "Let's not stay at hotels or eat at fancy restaurants. Let's just call on family and friends, the way folks used to do." And that's what we did. Mama let her long hair down, dressed herself in dainty sandals with skinny heels, big hoop earrings, and hip-hugging denim pedal pushers, and called on family and friends the whole trip.

I had never seen my mother look so brilliant; even the family and friends who gave us food and shelter along the way noticed how radiant she was. You could see it in their glances, in their smiles, in the quick double-takes some of the men chanced just to get a good behind glance of Mama in those tight denims—and, in the frowns on the faces of their wives when the men were caught.

While Mama seemed to flourish under the light of the attention she was getting during our travels that summer—years later, she would confess that turning fourty-four affected her the way turning fifty affects some women today—my father, on the other hand, seemed to deteriorate. He was not a bohemian; flitting from house to house was not his idea of fun. Daddy, who was not used to bad cooking, did not enjoy the uncertainty associated with visiting people whose cooking skills were a mystery up until the moment you took your first bite of something that they'd filled your plate with. Poor Daddy. Some of his culinary experiences on

Shortly after our arrival, we got a good whiff of the
could tell by the aroma alone that

the road trip were ghastly, like the cornbread that Mama's Cousin Aretha served; according to Daddy, it was so greasy, he might as well have eaten a block of lard that had been fried in fat—it gave him a heartburn that had him up and down all night. And the scorched orange pound cake that Miss Millicent Humphry—Mama's old high school teacher from New Orleans—tried to hide under a blanket of sugary-sweet whipped cream upset his stomach like nothing else.

Mama, despite the fact that she was going through her own little something, saw Daddy's distress and immediately tried to sweet-talk him back to good humor. She kept saying things like, "When we get to Elizabethtown you'll get a good meal" or "Miss Beatrice (Mama pronounced it Bee-at-trice) was one of the best cooks at Mercy Temple Church. On Big Sunday, people used to pass repeatedly by the table where she was setting out her goodies, just to get a whiff of her good cooking."

We were so grateful when we finally got to Elizabethtown, Kentucky. Mama had promised that we'd get a good meal there, but she hadn't said anything about how amazing Miss Beatrice Osborn, her former landlord, would be. Not only was Miss Bea an elegant host who cooked wonderful meals—we especially liked her walnut-raisin pie—she was well-spoken, sweet-mannered, had an equally well-spoken and sweet-mannered husband, Booker, and a grandson, Jimmy, who was the prettiest southern boy I had ever seen.

Shortly after our arrival, we got a good whiff of the dinner that was cooking in Miss Bea's oven and could tell by the aroma alone that we were in for something special. Miss Bea put a pipe in Daddy's mouth and sat him in a fat chair with an ottoman next to the one she had snuggled her husband inside, and insisted that Daddy lean back and not lift a finger. Soon after *dinner that was cooking in Miss Bea's oven and we were in for something special.*

I had laid eyes on her good-looking grandson, Jimmy, and saw that he was also laying eyes on me, Miss Bea said to me and Daddy, "I know Ruth's having a good time, but are the two of you enjoying your traipse along the back roads?"

"Yes," said Daddy, trying his best to sound high class, because that's how he thought he was supposed to sound in the company of such fine people. "We're calling this our Bohemian Adventure." I looked at Daddy, at Mama, at Miss Bea, and then at pretty Jimmy. "Yes," I said. "We're having a wonderful little traipse." I couldn't have been older than fourteen at the time.

- One 9-inch single Flaky Pie Crust (page 8), rolled out, fitted into a pie plate, and edge trimmed and crimped
- 3 large eggs
- ⅔ cup firmly packed dark brown sugar
- ¼ teaspoon salt
- ¼ cup (½ stick) unsalted butter, melted
- 1 cup light corn syrup
- 1 teaspoon vanilla extract
- 1 teaspoon grated orange rind
- ¼ teaspoon ground nutmeg
- 1 cup chopped walnuts
- 1 cup dark raisins

Makes one 9-inch pie

Preheat the oven to 375 degrees. Prepare the pie crust and set aside.

Crack the eggs over a large bowl. Add the brown sugar, salt, melted butter, and corn syrup and whisk together until well blended. Stir in the vanilla, orange rind, and nutmeg, then stir in the nuts and raisins. Pour the filling into the pie crust. Place in the oven and bake until the filling is set, 35 to 40 minutes; the pastry should be golden brown and a knife inserted in the center should come out clean. Let cool on a wire rack. Serve slightly warm or cool; either way, it tastes scrumptious with a dollop of whipped cream or a scoop of vanilla ice cream.

Cousin Eunice's Grated Carrot Pie

Mama said she got this recipe from Cousin Tillie, who said she got it from Aunt Bulah, who said she got it from Cousin Eunice, who said she copied it down out of the private collection of heirloom recipes owned by Miss Trimbley, a wealthy lady whose house Cousin Eunice—my maternal grandmother's cousin—was supposed to be cleaning while she was busy taking down recipes.

Unfortunately, by the time I came along, Cousin Eunice had been long gone, but her legendary meals remain as fresh on the minds of the people who'd been privy to them as they were on the days that she'd pulled one of them out of her oven. They say when she called you to supper, you didn't know what you were going to have, but you knew whatever it was, it wasn't going to be the ordinary garden variety supper that most country folks served. Cousin Eunice served things like Seafood Pilaf, Turkey Stroganoff, Polynesian Chicken, and Apple Tortes—pretty exotic sounding things to most people, who were used to gathering their entire meals from their backyards. If the truth be told, most of her recipes came from Miss Trimbley's

- One 9-inch single Flaky Pie Crust (page 8), rolled out, fitted into a pie plate, and edge trimmed and crimped
- 1¼ cups peeled and grated carrots
- ¾ cup sugar
- 1½ cups evaporated milk
- 3 large eggs, well beaten
- ¼ teaspoon ground nutmeg
- ¼ teaspoon ground cinnamon
- ⅛ teaspoon salt
- 1 teaspoon lemon extract

Makes one 9-inch pie

heirloom recipe collection. They say, Cousin Eunice had copied down so many of Miss Trimbley's recipes, she rarely cooked the same thing twice.

Mama used to say, "Some women'll tell you they don't need written instructions to tell them how to cook a good meal; they'll say, 'I could cook supper with my eyes blindfolded.' But I say, if you want a variety, if you want to serve more than beans and rice every day, there'll be times when you'll need to follow a recipe." No matter where you got it from.

Preheat the oven to 350 degrees. Prepare the pie crust and set aside.

In a large bowl, combine the carrots, sugar, and milk. Add the eggs and mix thoroughly. Add the nutmeg, cinnamon, salt, and lemon extract and blend well. Pour the filling into the crust, place in the oven, and bake until a knife inserted in the center comes out clean, 30 to 35 minutes. Let cool on a wire rack completely before serving.

Mary Bird Johnson's Golden Squash Pie

Growing up, there were two camps relative to catching a man—the *if-you-don't-chase-after-your-intended-some-other-woman-will* camp, to which Mama's friend Annabelle belonged, and the *if-you-start-off-running-after-a-man-you'll-always-be-running-after-him* camp, which Mama embraced. Annabelle would say, "Times're changing, women are pursuing what they want." Mama would answer, "Rules change, but human nature stays the same. A man will always prefer to do the chasing." Annabelle would counter, "While you've got your eye on the man you adore, waiting on him to do all the initiating, some fast tail woman'll come along and chase him straight to the altar." Mama would oppose, "That's why a woman should choose from the men who adore her; not the other way around. That way, she'll save herself a lot of running—you don't have to chase after a man who's already coming your way." I say, if you have a nice man coming your way, offering him a slice of my friend Mary Johnson's golden squash pie is a nice way to say, "Keep coming."

- One 9-inch single Flaky Pie Crust (page 8), rolled out, fitted into a pie plate, and edge trimmed and crimped
- ¾ cup sugar
- ½ teaspoon salt
- 1 teaspoon ground nutmeg
- ⅛ teaspoon ground ginger
- 1 cup mashed cooked yellow winter squash
- 3 large eggs
- 1 cup heavy cream
- ½ teaspoon lemon extract

Makes one 9-inch pie

Preheat the oven to 450 degrees. Prepare the pie crust and set aside.

In a medium-size bowl, blend together the sugar, salt, nutmeg, and ginger. Add the squash and mix completely. Crack the eggs, one at a time, into a separate medium-size bowl. Beat the eggs, then stir in the cream. Fold the egg mixture into the squash-spice mixture, making sure to thoroughly combine. Stir in the lemon extract. Pour the filling into the pie crust, place in the oven, and bake for 10 minutes, then reduce the oven temperature to 350 degrees and bake until a knife inserted in the center comes out clean, another 35 to 40 minutes. Let cool completely on a wire rack, then doll up each serving with a spoonful of vanilla ice cream.

Patty Walker's Easy Nut and Chips Pie

My insightful mother challenged the old adage, "Half of a man is better than no man at all." Mama used to say, "You want more than just breath and britches. You want a man who'll stop by and sit with you a while, take you to the movies, to dinner, and on slow drives through town."

My jet-setting hairdresser, Patty, who at one time dressed the heads of funk masters Rick James and George Clinton, enjoys darting in and out of town, dolling up, and flitting from one event to the other. In the beauty shop, Patty says, "Sometimes, 'half' of the man is all a woman has time for—or wants to be bothered with." With that, the women in the shop laugh, slap each other a high five, and say, "Girl, I know that's right!"

- One 9-inch single Flaky Pie Crust (page 8), rolled out, fitted into a pie plate, and edge trimmed and crimped
- ½ cup (1 stick) unsalted butter, softened
- 1 cup sugar
- ½ cup all-purpose flour
- 2 large eggs
- 1 teaspoon vanilla extract
- 1 cup coarsely chopped pecans
- 1 cup semisweet chocolate chips
- ½ cup butterscotch chips

Makes one 9-inch pie

Preheat the oven to 350 degrees. Prepare the pie crust and set aside.

Combine the butter, sugar, flour, eggs, and vanilla in a large bowl and beat until blended well with an electric mixer. Stir in the pecans, chocolate chips, and butterscotch chips. Pour the filling into the pie crust. Place in the oven and bake until the crust turns golden, about 40 minutes. Let cool completely on a wire rack before serving. You can dress up each slice with a spoonful of vanilla ice cream or fresh whipped cream.

Redemption Hazelnut Pie

Long before John Gray told us that men are from Mars and women are from Venus, Mama used to say, *Men are from a different place. Some things about us, they just don't understand.* Like the time Daddy went out and bought Mama a hardwood floor buffer for their anniversary. Daddy just couldn't understand why, for the next few days, Mama walked around the house giving him the silent treatment. Eventually, she asked Daddy how he'd feel if she'd given him a snow shovel or a push broom. Daddy got the picture and promptly went out and bought Mama a gorgeous pearl necklace. The next day, Mama baked him the hazelnut pie that he liked so much.

- One 9-inch single Flaky Pie Crust (page 8), rolled out, fitted into a pie plate, and edge trimmed and crimped
- 3 large eggs
- ½ cup firmly packed light brown sugar
- 1 cup dark corn syrup
- ⅛ teaspoon salt
- 1 teaspoon vanilla extract
- ¼ cup (½ stick) unsalted butter, melted
- 1½ cups roasted hazelnuts, finely chopped

Makes one 9-inch pie

Preheat the oven to 350 degrees. Prepare the pie crust and set aside.

In a medium-size bowl, lightly beat the eggs just until blended. Add the brown sugar, corn syrup, salt, and vanilla, then stir in the melted butter and hazelnuts. Pour the filling into the pie crust, place in the oven, and bake until a knife inserted in the center comes out clean, 45 to 50 minutes. Let cool completely on a wire rack before serving.

Linda Lewis's Pumpkin-Coconut Pie

When I was a little girl, Mama used to tell me, "I couldn't stay with a man who was constantly standing over my shoulder, always complaining about something: Do you really need all of these shoes? . . . You just talked to your mother an hour ago . . . When you gonna iron my shirts? . . .We just had chicken the other day. A finicky man will work you to the bone, if you let him."

Mama used to tell me, "In this world, there'll always be somebody reaching out for something. But you can't let other people's needs control you. You can't do for others, and not do for yourself."

For over 30 years, Mama had a time of day that belonged exclusively to her. Between ten and eleven o'clock in the morning, Daddy knew that Mama would be perched on a stool at the kitchen counter listening to a radio recipe exchange show called "Listen to The Mrs." During that hour, Daddy allowed Mama to have her private time; if he wanted a glass of ice water or a towel to wash his car with, he got it himself. In retrospect, I guess Daddy did benefit from Mama listening to the recipe show, because many of her wonderful recipes were a result of it.

Linda Lewis, who is married to Art Lewis, the host of the "Listen to the Mrs." show, says the addition of coconut in her pumpkin pies adds a little frou-frou to the standard version.

Mama used to tell me, "I couldn't stay with a man who was constantly standing over my shoulder, always complaining about something....A finicky man will work you to the bone, if you let him."

- One 9-inch single Flaky Pie Crust (page 8), rolled out, fitted into a pie plate, and edge trimmed and crimped
- 2 cups cooked, drained, and mashed fresh pumpkin (canned works fine, too)
- ½ cup sugar
- ½ cup molasses
- 3 large eggs
- 1¼ cups whole milk
- ½ cup evaporated milk
- ½ teaspoon ground cinnamon
- ¼ teaspoon salt
- 1 tablespoon cornstarch
- 2 tablespoons unsalted butter, melted
- 1 cup sweetened shredded coconut

Makes one 9-inch pie

Preheat the oven to 350 degrees. Prepare the pie crust and set aside.

In a large bowl, combine the pumpkin, sugar, and molasses thoroughly. Gently beat in the eggs. Pour in the milk and evaporated milk. Stir in the cinnamon, salt, cornstarch, and melted butter, blending together well. Fold in the coconut. Pour the filling into the pie crust, place in the oven, and bake until the center is set, 1 to 1¼ hours. Let cool completely on a wire rack.

Serve each slice topped with a dollop of fresh whipped cream.

Mama's Zucchini Cobbler

My mother's zucchini cobbler recipe was a shining example of the wonderful things that she could create from the garden gifts that people gave her. Mama used to say, "When people give you something, don't just say 'thank you' show 'thank you'."

It used to stroke Mama's ego when she would give somebody a helping of her zucchini cobbler and they'd carry on so because they couldn't believe she had taken a garden vegetable and made something out of it that tasted just like apple pie—to many people, it tasted better. The first time Mr. Youngblood (one of Mama's renters) tasted it, he said, "Dawlin', if you wasn't already tooken, I'd marry you this eve'nin." Looking back, and knowing how giddy old men get when they're in the presence of a pretty, young woman, I suspect he meant every word of it.

- Dough for one 9 x 13-inch double Flaky Pie Crust (page 8)
- 4 medium-size zucchini, peeled, seeded, and sliced the way you slice apples for apple pie (7 to 8 cups of ½-inch slices)

FILLING

- ½ cup distilled white vinegar
- ¼ cup fresh lemon juice
- 1 cup granulated sugar
- ½ cup firmly packed light brown sugar
- ½ cup all-purpose flour
- 1 teaspoon ground cinnamon
- 1 teaspoon ground nutmeg
- 1 tablespoon vanilla extract
- ¼ teaspoon salt
- 3 tablespoons unsalted butter, cut into bits

GLAZE TOPPING

- 1 large egg white
- 1 tablespoon water
- 1 teaspoon granulated sugar

Makes one 9 x 13-inch cobbler

Preheat the oven to 350 degrees. Divide the dough into two disks, making one slightly larger than the other; set them aside.

In a large bowl, combine the zucchini, vinegar, and lemon juice, tossing until well combined. Let the mixture marinate for 35 to 40 minutes at room temperature.

In a separate bowl, sift together both sugars, the flour, cinnamon, and nutmeg. Stir the vanilla and salt into the zucchini mixture. Pour the sugar mixture into the zucchini mixture and gently toss together until the zucchini slices are well coated.

On a lightly floured work surface, roll out the larger disk of dough into a 12 x 16-inch rectangle. Fit it into a 9 x 13-inch baking dish. The edges should hang about 1½ inches beyond the dish. Pour the zucchini filling into the crust and dot with the butter. Roll out the top crust to a 10 x 14-inch rectangle and place it on top of the pie. There should be about a ½-inch overhang of dough. Gather the top and bottom crust edges together and fold the top crust under the bottom crust. Crimp the edges with the tines of a fork. Cut a few steam vents in the top crust.

In a small bowl, beat the egg white and water together until foamy. Using a pastry brush, brush the crust with the glaze, then sprinkle it with the sugar. Place in the oven and bake until the crust is golden and the filling bubbly, 35 to 40 minutes. Let cool on a wire rack at least 10 to 15 minutes before serving.

Miss Claudette Cotton's White Potato Pie

Miss Claudette got around. While the other housewives in our neighborhood were at their front doors in pink hair rollers and red bandannas, waving goodbye to their husbands who were backing out of their driveways on their way to work, Miss Claudette was fully dressed and waiting in the car—in the driver's seat—and honking the horn for her husband Russell to get a move on. We could hear her yelling, "You gonna be late for work and I'm gonna be late for my hair appointment." Russell, a tall bean pole of a man, would come stumbling out the door and hop into the passenger side of the car, then Miss Claudette would take off like a rocket. For the rest of the day, while the other housewives in our neighborhood were confined to their houses, Miss Claudette was coming and going as she pleased.

Daddy didn't care for Miss Claudette. He would say things to Mama like, "She smokes, she curses, she wears her skirts too tight; I don't think you ought to be around a woman like that." Sometimes, Mama would plead a case, "I only went to the store with her; we drove to Bay City to pick berries, that's all; she doesn't smoke and curse around me." Other times Mama would tell Daddy, "I think I'm old enough to choose my own friends."

One 9-inch single Flaky Pie Crust (page 8), rolled out, fitted into a pie plate, and edge trimmed and crimped

2 medium-size white potatoes (russet or Idaho for a light, fluffy texture, or Yukon Gold or Yellow Finn for a smooth and creamy texture—both ways are good)

¼ cup (½ stick) unsalted butter, softened

1 cup sugar

½ teaspoon baking powder

⅛ teaspoon salt

½ cup milk

½ cup heavy cream

1 teaspoon vanilla extract

1 teaspoon lemon extract

⅛ teaspoon ground nutmeg

3 large eggs, beaten

Makes one 9-inch pie

Once, when I was a little girl, Mama and I spent the whole day riding around with Miss Claudette. Daddy was right: Miss Claudette smoked, she cursed, and her skirt was way too tight. But we had the most wonderful girly time; Miss Claudette honked her horn at the cute men we drove past and, when one blew kisses, she blew kisses back. At times, Mama, who was usually prim and proper, slid down in her seat and hid her face in the palms of her hands; other times, she laughed so hard, tears spilled down her cheeks. "Claudette, you are something else," she cried.

When we got home, Mama didn't say, don't tell your daddy where we've been or who we've been with, she just said, "It's not good to let a man tell you who you can or cannot be friends with." I agreed with Mama. To this day, I have never mentioned a thing to Daddy about the day that Mama and I spent carousing around town with Miss Claudette.

I don't think Miss Claudette spent a lot of time in the kitchen. How could she? She spent most of the day jetting in and out of her driveway. But every now and then—after Daddy had gone to work—she would stop over with a covered dish. "Tell me how you like this cake (or these cookies . . . or this pie)." She would say, "I went way beyond my budget this week; bought me some new shoes (or a new dress or a piece of jewelry) and I need something to soften the news when I tell Russell." We really liked her white potato pie, and we told her so.

Preheat the oven to 350 degrees. Prepare the pie crust and set aside.

Peel the potatoes, cut into chunks, and cook in boiling water until tender; drain. In a medium-size bowl, mash the potatoes and combine with the butter, sugar, baking powder, and salt until well mixed. Stir in the milk and cream, stirring until well blended. Stir in the extracts, then the nutmeg. Add the eggs and mix well. Pour the filling into the pie crust, place in the oven, and bake until a knife inserted in the center comes out clean, about 45 minutes. Let cool completely on a wire rack. Top each slice with a scoop of lemon-flavored ice cream for added flair and extra flavor.

Sweet Potato Pie (Cousin Caldin's Rendition)

All of the women in my family make different versions of this southern classic. Some season their pies with lots of different spices, like cinnamon, nutmeg, and cloves. Some add a little buttermilk and molasses to give theirs that deep, down-home flavor. Others get fancy with nuts and crumb toppings. My great-grandmother's cousin Sue used to slip a little corn liquor in her pies. Well, truth be told, Cousin Sue used to slip a little corn liquor in just about everything.

My beautiful cousin Caldin Street, who still provides glitzy, show-stopping entertainment via her 1960s girly singing group, The Velvelettes, exudes an exquisitely hypnotic feminine style not only on stage, but also in her kitchen. Cal, who can strut right off a stage and straight into a kitchen—still wearing sequins and feather boas—makes the transition look easy. Cousin Cal says, "A woman has many sides."

Caldin's lightly seasoned sweet potato pies are the best. As far as I'm concerned, her pie baking skills emanate from her finest side.

- One 9-inch single Flaky Pie Crust (page 8), rolled out, fitted into a pie plate, and edge trimmed and crimped
- 3 hand-sized sweet potatoes
- 2 large eggs
- 1½ cups sugar
- 1 teaspoon lemon extract
- ¼ teaspoon salt
- ½ teaspoon ground nutmeg
- ½ cup (1 stick) unsalted butter, melted
- ½ cup evaporated milk

Makes one 9-inch pie

Preheat the oven to 350 degrees. Prepare the pie crust and set aside.

Place the potatoes in a medium-size saucepan, cover generously with water, bring to a boil and cook until fork-tender. Drain and, when they've cooled enough to handle, peel and mash them in a large bowl until there are no lumps remaining. Using a fork, remove any strings from the filling. (If you're using an electric mixer, remove any strings that might have collected around the beaters.) Add the eggs, sugar, lemon extract, salt, and nutmeg and beat together until thoroughly blended and smooth. Add the melted butter and evaporated milk and beat until creamy. Pour the filling into the pie crust.

Place the pie in the oven and bake until the center is set (it shouldn't jiggle when the pie is gently rocked back and forth) and the crust golden brown, about 45 minutes. Let cool completely on a wire rack. As far as I'm concerned, sweet potato pie tastes best at room temperature. You can serve it garnished with whipped cream or pecan halves, but I prefer mine plain.

7

Meringue Pies

I've seen some of the most ordinary-looking women fix themselves up to look breathtaking. Most times, it had everything to do with the attractive way they adorned themselves when they finished dressing—a silk scarf tied ever so nicely, just enough bangles on the arm to send out the right chime, a striking fragrance to draw out the inner beauty. The right embellishment has a way of taking something ordinary and making it superb.

When I was going through a divorce and approaching thirty, I found myself at a place where I felt myself fading. My feminine sense of self was being challenged at every turn: my girly looks were maturing and my handsome ex-husband had already gone out and found himself a bevy of gorgeous Friday night dates. The situation looked blue; I looked blue.

All the while, my mother had her eye on me. "It's alright to have a good cry, as long as you do it in the privacy of your own home, but when you get through crying, look up and get up," she would say. Patiently, Mama waited for me to stop sulking. And when I did, she bought me a full-length mink coat and my Aunt Helen bought me a mink jacket. That summer, the women in my family—my mother, my Aunt Helen, and my cousins Azure and Machon—treated me to a weeklong Caribbean cruise. Thanks to them (they had bought me a trunk full of island wear), I felt like The Girl from Ipanema. Mama kept saying, "You're young and you're attractive; you're at the age where you still can go forward and become whatever you want to become."

Mama was beside herself with hope for me. She beamed with pride whenever I emerged from my cabin dripping with womanly accessories. When an older, wealthy-looking gentleman admirer set his sights on me, Mama watched his movements like a hawk. When he said to Mama, "Your daughter's somethin' else," Mama didn't stall or play coy. She stuck her chest out, looked him directly in the eye, and proclaimed, "She certainly is!"

I learned a lot that summer. Sometimes all you need are a few lustrous trimmings to help you get your groove back and reconnect with your womanish.

The same goes for pies. Sometimes you can change the entire appearance and taste of a pie simply by embellishing it with a little meringue top.

Daddy's Mother's Blueberry Meringue Pie

Even though Mama didn't speak about Grandmother (Daddy's mother) in the glowing way that Daddy did when he reminisced about his mother—Mama did say some sweet things about her mother-in-law. Mama lauded her for the lovable way that Grandmother treated her, even though Mama knew (through Grandmother's lovable and subtle hinting) that she hadn't been Grandmother's first choice for Daddy; a pretty, brown-skinned girl named Ora Faye had. Mama spoke sweetly of Grandmother's quilting; she said Grandmother's quilts were pretty enough to hang in the Smithsonian. And that you had to go some to outdo her in the kitchen; said her pies could win ribbons. Grandmother used to blush underneath all of that sweet talk Mama heaped on her. Eventually, she stopped touting Ora Faye's virtues and started praising Mama's.

Mama used to say, "Sweet talk will do more for you than a whip."

One 9-inch single Flaky Pie Crust (page 8), rolled out, fitted into a pie plate, edge trimmed and crimped, and partially prebaked (page 9)

FILLING

¾ cup sugar

¼ cup all-purpose flour

¼ teaspoon ground cinnamon

2 teaspoons grated lemon rind

4½ cups fresh blueberries, picked over

1 tablespoon fresh lemon juice

2 tablespoons unsalted butter, cut into small pieces

MERINGUE

3 large egg whites, at room temperature

¼ teaspoon cream of tartar

⅓ cup sugar

Makes one 9-inch pie

Preheat the oven to 350 degrees. Prepare the pie crust and partially prebake. Set aside on a wire rack.

Make the filling. Combine the sugar, flour, cinnamon, and lemon rind in a large bowl. Gently stir in the blueberries and lemon juice until the berries are well coated. Pour the filling into the pie crust, dot with the butter, place in the oven, and bake for 30 minutes

Meanwhile, make the meringue. In a medium-size bowl using an electric mixer, beat together the egg whites and cream of tartar until soft peaks form when the beaters are raised. Gradually add the sugar, beating well after each addition. Continue to beat until shiny, stiff peaks form when the beaters are raised.

Take the pie out of the oven. Mound the meringue in the center of the pie, then spread it evenly around the edge of the inner crust, sealing the meringue to the crust. Use a spoon to create a design of peaks and valleys all over the meringue. Put the pie back in the oven and bake until the meringue is nicely browned, another 10 to 15 minutes. Let cool completely on a wire rack before serving.

Carolyn Bennett's Grandmother's Key Lime Pie

My friend Carolyn Bennett is tall, educated, and culturally astute. At least once a year we meet in Chicago and spend a whirlwind weekend perusing world-class museums and chic art galleries. In 1995 Carolyn was included in *Who's Who of American Women,* an impressive accomplishment for a woman who lost her mother when she was five years old. Carolyn once told me that, after her mother died, she was sent to live with her maternal grandmother; said she'd been told that her father was dead. Said, her grandmother, who was overwhelmed with the prospect of raising a small child, was distant, at best. Carolyn says she spent a lot of time sitting alone on her grandmother's front porch. Said, on her way to the porch, her grandmother would always say, "Do not talk to the old woman who lives next door."

One day, while Carolyn was sitting on the steps, Mrs. Strong, the old neighbor woman, came to her door and invited Carolyn over for a slice of Key lime pie. The invitation was too good to turn down. She couldn't help herself and crept across the yard. Once inside Mrs. Strong's immaculate kitchen, Carolyn was given a seat in an old rocking chair and a huge piece of pie. Mrs. Strong asked Carolyn about school and life in general. Carolyn said she felt a great sense of love and comfort; sort of like being in the presence of an angel. Soon, Carolyn was sneaking over regularly to Mrs. Strong's for conversation and Key lime pie. Each time, the old woman

would beckon little Carolyn to the rocking chair, cut her a lovely slice of pie, and talk to her about the things that mattered to her. My friend said that one day while she was rocking and eating pie, her beloved Mrs. Strong confessed, "I am your grandmother," she said. "I'm your father's mother. Years ago our families had a falling out and I promised to remain silent about my true identity. But not any more."

According to Carolyn, from that day forward, her life changed. Said, she began visiting Mrs. Strong on a regular basis. Said, she'd sit in the old rocking chair, talking and laughing, and eating her grandmother's delicious Key lime pie.

One 9-inch single Flaky Pie Crust (page 8), rolled out, fitted into a pie plate, and edge trimmed and crimped

FILLING

1¼ cups sugar

¼ cup all-purpose flour

3 tablespoons cornstarch

¼ teaspoon salt

2 cups water

3 large egg yolks

⅓ cup Key lime juice, bottled or fresh

1 tablespoon grated lime rind

2 tablespoons unsalted butter

A few drops of green food coloring (optional)

MERINGUE

3 large egg whites, at room temperature

½ teaspoon vanilla extract

¼ cup sugar

Makes one 9-inch pie

Preheat the oven to 425 degrees. Prepare the pie crust and fully prebake. Set aside on a wire rack.

Make the filling. In a medium-size saucepan, combine the sugar, flour, cornstarch, and salt, then gradually whisk in the water. Over medium heat, bring to a boil, stirring constantly, and continue to boil, whisking, until the mixture thickens, about 2 minutes. Remove from the heat.

In a medium-size bowl, beat the egg yolks until thick and lemon colored. Slowly add about one-quarter of the hot sugar mixture to the egg yolks, beating constantly. Pour the egg yolk mixture into the saucepan. Return the saucepan to low heat and cook for 2 minutes, stirring constantly. Remove from the heat and whisk in the lime juice and rind and the butter. Stir in a few drops of green food coloring, if you desire, and stir until the butter melts and everything is well combined. Pour the filling into the pie crust. Set aside.

Make the meringue. In a medium-size bowl, using an electric mixer, beat the egg whites until they form soft peaks. Add the vanilla and gradually add the sugar, continuing to beat until shiny, stiff peaks form. Mound the meringue in the center of the pie, then spread it evenly around the edge of the inner crust, sealing the meringue to the crust. Use a spoon to create a design of peaks and valleys all over the meringue. Place in the oven and bake until the meringue is nice and golden, 6 to 7 minutes. Let cool completely on a wire rack, then chill in the refrigerator for at least 2 hours before serving.

Almeta McCray's Tangerine Meringue Pie

For a city girl, my friend Almeta gives the best down-home advice. She says, when it comes to men, we women spend way too much time sizing up one another. She says, "You can't be all things to all men, the way a big department store offers a little bit of this, and a little bit of that. Instead of rivaling with each other, every woman ought to think of herself as a little boutique. She ought to concentrate on the thing that she does best, and specialize in that."

Almeta's advice says it all and so does her lovely tangerine meringue pie.

One 9-inch single Flaky Pie Crust (page 8), rolled out, fitted into a pie plate, and edge trimmed and crimped

FILLING

1¼ cups sugar

3 tablespoons cornstarch

⅛ teaspoon salt

½ cup fresh tangerine juice (from 4 to 6 tangerines)

4 large egg yolks

1 teaspoon finely grated tangerine rind

¼ cup (½ stick) unsalted butter, melted

MERINGUE

4 to 6 large egg whites (depending on how high you want your meringue), at room temperature

½ cup sugar

Make one 9-inch pie

Preheat the oven to 350 degrees. Prepare the pie crust and fully prebake. Set aside on a wire rack.

Make the filling. In a large saucepan, combine the sugar, cornstarch, and salt. Gradually whisk in the tangerine juice until smooth. Whisk in the egg yolks until thoroughly combined. Stir in the tangerine rind and butter.

Cook over medium heat, whisking constantly, and gradually reduce the heat as the filling begins to bubble and thicken; this will take 8 to 10 minutes. Remove from the heat and pour the hot filling into the pie crust. Set aside.

Make the meringue. In a medium-size bowl, using an electric mixer, beat the egg whites on medium speed until foamy. Add the sugar, 1 tablespoon at a time, and beat on high speed after each addition until dissolved, then until the egg whites form shiny, stiff peaks. Mound the meringue in the center of the pie, then spread it evenly around the edge of the inner crust. Use a spoon to create a design of peaks and valleys all over the meringue. Place in the oven and bake until the peaks are nicely browned, 8 to 10 minutes. Let cool on a wire rack for 1 hour, then refrigerate for at least 3 hours before serving.

Old-Time Chocolate Meringue Pie

One 9-inch single Flaky Pie Crust (page 8), rolled out, fitted into a pie plate, and edge trimmed and crimped

FILLING

3 large eggs yolks

¼ cup (½ stick) unsalted butter

⅓ cup unsweetened cocoa powder

One 14-ounce can sweetened condensed milk

½ cup water

1 teaspoon vanilla extract

MERINGUE

3 large egg whites

¼ teaspoon cream of tartar

½ teaspoon vanilla extract

¼ cup sugar

Makes one 9-inch pie

My mother used to say, "Young women today don't understand the power that's available to them, right there in their kitchens. They think the only way to hold onto a man is to buy something skimpy from the lingerie shop. I admit everything that's required to feed a man can't be found inside your pantry, but I'm here to tell you, you can save a lot of money if you look there first. 'Cause what you buy at the lingerie shop, a man sees all the time. But a nice, little chocolate meringue pie made from scratch? Well, that's something a man's not gonna see everywhere."

Preheat the oven to 350 degrees. Prepare the pie crust and fully prebake. Set aside on a wire rack.

Make the filling. Beat the yolks until well blended, then set aside. Heat the butter in a medium-size saucepan over low heat until it melts. Add the cocoa, condensed milk, and water and stir constantly with a large spoon or a wire whisk until smooth. Stir in the yolks and the vanilla until smooth and thickened. Remove from the heat. Beat out any lumps that might have formed. Pour the filling into the pie crust.

Make the meringue. Combine the egg whites, cream of tartar, and vanilla in a medium-size bowl and beat with an electric mixer until soft peaks form. Add the sugar 1 tablespoon at a time and continue beating until shiny, stiff peaks form and all of the sugar has dissolved. Mound in the center of the pie, then spread it evenly around the edge of the inner crust, sealing the meringue to the crust. Use a spoon to create a design of peaks and valleys all over the meringue. Bake until the meringue is golden, 8 to 10 minutes. Let cool completely on a wire rack.

Fabulous Mile-High Lemon Meringue Pie

I know the magazines say it's sort of tawdry to have your girly things sitting out on display. They say things like creams and gels and salves and vials of scented oils should be put away in discreet little places. However, sometimes I like to exhibit my most exotic ointments; especially the ones in the ultra-feminine containers. I like to give the impression that I'm the kind of woman who spoils herself with lavish emoluments.

My mother used to say, *People'll treat you the way they see you treating yourself.*

If the truth be told, I play the same kinds of little games when something I've cooked turns out good-looking. I won't hesitate to flaunt an attractive dish, knowing full well that I've got it sitting on the table or on the countertop, to bring attention to myself. What more can I say? Everybody enjoys a little time under the light.

For the purpose of showing off, there isn't a pie more beautiful than a sweet, mile-high lemon meringue pie; it just looks so ladylike.

One 9-inch single Flaky Pie Crust (page 8), rolled out, fitted into a pie plate, and edge trimmed and crimped

FILLING

- ¼ cup cornstarch
- 3 tablespoons sifted cake flour
- 1¾ cups sugar
- ¼ teaspoon salt
- 2 cups whole milk
- 4 large egg yolks
- ½ cup fresh lemon juice (from 2 to 3 medium-size lemons)
- 1 tablespoon grated lemon rind
- 2 tablespoons unsalted butter, softened

Preheat the oven to 350 degrees. Prepare the pie crust and fully prebake. Set aside on a wire rack.

Make the filling. Combine the cornstarch, flour, sugar, and salt in a medium-size, heavy saucepan. Gradually whisk in the milk until the cornstarch is dissolved and the mixture smooth. Over medium heat, slowly bring to a boil, whisking constantly. Let it continue to boil, whisking, until it thickens, 3 to 4 minutes. Remove from the heat.

In a medium-size bowl, whisk the egg yolks until thick and lemon colored. Gradually whisk about one-fourth of the hot mixture into the yolks. Slowly pour the egg yolk mixture into the saucepan and whisk until smooth. Return the saucepan to low heat and cook for 5 minutes, whisking

I won't hesitate to flaunt an attractive dish, knowing full well that I've got it sitting on the table or on the countertop, to bring attention to myself.

constantly, then remove from the heat. Stir in the lemon juice and rind and the butter until thoroughly combined. Wait about 5 minutes, then cover the filling with plastic wrap to prevent a skin from forming on top. Set the pan aside.

Make the meringue. In a medium-size bowl using an electric mixer, beat the egg whites, cream of tartar, and salt together until soft peaks form. Beat in the sugar in a slow stream until it is completely dissolved. Add the vanilla and continue beating until shiny, stiff peaks form.

Pour the filling into the pie crust. Mound the meringue in the center of the pie, then spread it evenly around the edge of the inner crust, sealing the meringue to the crust. Use a spoon to create a design of peaks and valleys all over the meringue. Bake until the meringue is golden brown, 8 to 10 minutes. Let cool completely before serving. Right about now, I'd start thinking of some excuse to call someone over and casually draw their attention to the beautiful pie cooling on my counter.

MERINGUE

4 large egg whites, at room temperature

½ teaspoon cream of tartar

⅛ teaspoon salt

½ cup sugar

1 teaspoon vanilla extract

Makes one 9-inch pie

Old-Fashioned Apple Meringue Pie

Family lore has it that when my daddy's grandmother was a little girl, she went to town in response to an announcement made by the daughters of an elderly woman who were looking for someone to cook and clean for their mother. When my grandmother got to the house, the old woman took an immediate liking to her, but they say the woman's daughters had to be won over. Say, the daughters gave my grandmother a dust cloth and a straw broom to see what she could do; say, they were in awe as they stood back and watched that little girl clean the woman's house just as good as any woman could've.

They tell me, that even after my grandmother gave that old lady's house a cleaning it had never had, one of the daughters continued to have doubts: "After all," she said, "You're still just a child. Can you cook? We're having company this evening. My sister and I are gonna stuff a turkey. Do you know how to pare potatoes?" Say, the sisters led my grandmother to the kitchen and, once there, Grandmother found the fruit trees in the backyard. They say Grandmother

commenced to making the best looking apple pie—replete with a meringue on top of it—that the sisters had ever seen. Say, soon after Grandmother slipped the pie in the oven, she turned to the sisters, just as nonchalant, and said, "Now, go fetch me that turkey."

When my mother was teaching me how to cook, she used to say, "When you cook you can't be shy; you've got to show the pots that you're the boss."

One 9-inch single Flaky Pie Crust (page 8), rolled out, fitted into a pie plate, and edge trimmed and crimped

FILLING

⅔ cup sugar

3 tablespoons unsalted butter, softened

1 tablespoon fresh lemon juice

3 large egg yolks, beaten

2½ cups peeled, cored, and coarsely grated apples (any baking apple will do: Golden Delicious, Gold Rush, Suncrisp, Pink Lady)

½ teaspoon ground cinnamon

½ teaspoon ground nutmeg

MERINGUE

3 large egg whites, at room temperature

¼ cup sugar

½ teaspoon vanilla extract

Makes one 9-inch pie

Preheat the oven to 350 degrees. Prepare the pie crust and set aside.

Make the filling. In a medium-size bowl, cream together the sugar and butter. Blend in the lemon juice and egg yolks. Gently fold in the grated apples until well combined. Pour the filling into the pie crust and sprinkle the top evenly with the cinnamon and nutmeg. Place in the oven and bake until the apples are nice and tender, 40 to 45 minutes.

Meanwhile, make the meringue. In a medium-size bowl, using an electric mixer, beat the egg whites until foamy. Add in the sugar, 1 tablespoon at a time, beating well after each addition, and continue to beat until shiny, stiff peaks form. Briefly beat in the vanilla.

Take the pie out of the oven. Mound the meringue in the center of the pie, then spread it evenly around the edge of the inner crust, sealing the meringue to the crust. Use a spoon to create a design of peaks and valleys all over the meringue. Put the pie back in the oven and bake until the meringue is light golden, 8 to 10 minutes. Let cool on a wire rack. This pie can be served warm or cold.

Miss Annie Dugan's Grape Juice Meringue Pie

If I could, I would honor each of the women who strive to keep me looking good with their own special day: Miss Patty Walker, my hairstylist; Kat, who does my manicures and pedicures; and Miss Annie Dugan, my Mary Kay lady.

I'd probably set aside two days of tribute for Miss Annie (who once told me, "Never underrate the power of keeping yourself well-groomed, 'cause an ordinary looking but impeccably groomed woman can stand next to a beauty queen and look just as striking"). Not only does she keep me looking good with a steady supply of lipstick and mascara and inner beauty advice, she's also the source of a lot of the recipes in my collection that have caused people at family gatherings and community potlucks to gather around and make a fuss over the dish that I've brought to pass. And you know that's right up my alley.

One 9-inch single Flaky Pie Crust (page 8), rolled out, fitted into a pie plate, and edge trimmed and crimped

FILLING

3 large egg yolks

¾ cup sugar

¼ cup cornstarch

2 cups Concord grape juice

2 tablespoon unsalted butter

2 teaspoons fresh lemon juice

MERINGUE

3 large egg whites

⅛ teaspoon salt

⅓ cup sugar

Makes one 9-inch pie

Preheat the oven to 350 degrees. Prepare the pie crust and fully prebake. Set aside.

Make the filling. Place the egg yolks in a medium-size bowl and set aside. Mix the sugar and cornstarch in a medium-size, heavy saucepan. Stir in the grape juice and cook over medium heat, whisking constantly, until the mixture boils and thickens, 1 to 2 minutes. Remove from the heat.

Beat the egg yolks lightly, then whisk at least half of the hot mixture into them. Pour the egg yolk mixture into the saucepan, place back over medium heat, and let boil for 1 minute, whisking constantly. Remove from the heat and stir in the butter and lemon juice until completely combined. Pour the filling into the pie crust.

Make the meringue. In a medium-size bowl, using an electric mixer, beat the egg whites and salt together until foamy. Gradually beat in the sugar until shiny, stiff peaks form. Mound the meringue in the center of the pie, then spread it along the edge of the inner crust, sealing it to the crust. Use a spoon to create a design of peaks and valleys all over the meringue. Bake until the peaks are golden brown, 12 to 15 minutes. Let cool on a wire rack before serving.

Miss Cooper's Banana Pudding Pie

One of my favorite photos is of Mama coming in from her garden. And while the photo is not her most flattering picture—her hair's torn up and she's wearing a pair of muddy, clunky-looking shoes—I cherish it just the same, because Mama's garden was her pride and joy. She had an amazing green thumb and could grow just about anything. People were always pinching off pieces of flowers and plants and saying, "Take this sprout, Ruth. I know it'll flourish under your care."

In addition to beans, okra, tomatoes, and peas, zinnias, petunias, marigolds, and bachelor buttons, Mama also grew lifelong friendships in her garden. Miss Cooper, whose lush garden was adjacent to Mama's, was Mama's best garden friend. When the two of them met up at the far end of their respective adjoining gardens, they would spend hours talking about flowers and plants and exchanging recipes. When I was a little girl, I could look out the kitchen window and see them standing down a long, straight row, grinning and nodding. Watching the two of them, I couldn't wait to grow up and have a garden friend like Miss Cooper. I saw my garden friend and myself sitting in a beautiful garden, wearing beautiful hats, sipping tea, eating fancy little treats, and saying things like, "I do say, aren't the beans and the okra and the tomatoes and the peas and the zinnias and the petunias and the marigolds and the bachelor buttons coming out nicely this year?" Mama always kept a pad and a pencil in her garden apron pocket; she said Miss Cooper gave out the most wonderful recipes.

CRUST

1½ cups finely crushed vanilla wafers

2 tablespoons sugar

⅛ teaspoon salt

5 tablespoons unsalted butter, melted and slightly cooled

½ teaspoon vanilla extract

FILLING

¾ cup sugar

3 tablespoons cornstarch

1 vanilla bean

1 cup heavy cream

1 cup whole milk

3 large egg yolks, lightly beaten

½ teaspoon vanilla extract

3 tablespoons unsalted butter, melted and slightly cooled

2 firm, ripe bananas, peeled and thinly sliced

About 1 cup whole vanilla wafers

MERINGUE

3 large egg whites

½ teaspoon vanilla extract

¼ teaspoon cream of tartar

⅓ cup sugar

Makes one 9-inch pie

Preheat the oven to 350 degrees.

Make the crust. Combine the crust ingredients in a medium-size bowl and stir until the crumbs are evenly moistened. Firmly press the mixture into the bottom and up the sides to the rim of a 9-inch pie plate, forming a crust. Place in the oven and bake until golden and crisp, 8 to 10 minutes. Let cool on a wire rack.

Make the filling. Combine the sugar and cornstarch in a medium-size bowl. Using the tip of a paring knife, split the vanilla bean lengthwise and scrape out the inner seeds from both sides of the bean with the edge of the knife. Whisk the seeds into the sugar mixture, then slowly beat in the cream, then the milk in a thin, steady stream. Whisk in the egg yolks one at a time. Transfer the mixture to a medium-size, heavy saucepan and cook over low to medium heat, whisking constantly and gently, until it thickens, about 8 minutes. Remove from the heat and whisk in the vanilla and melted butter until thoroughly combined.

Arrange the sliced bananas over the bottom crust. Pour half the pudding over the bananas, spreading it evenly with a rubber spatula. Arrange a single layer of whole vanilla wafers on top of the pudding. Pour the remaining pudding over the wafers and spread it evenly with the spatula. Place in the refrigerator and chill for 12 to 15 minutes.

Meanwhile, make the meringue. In a medium-size bowl, using an electric mixer, beat together the egg whites, vanilla, and cream of tartar until soft peaks form. Gradually add the sugar, 1 tablespoon at a time, beating continually until the sugar is completely dissolved and shiny, stiff peaks form.

Mound the meringue in the center of the pie, then spread it evenly around the edge of the inner crust, sealing the meringue to the crust. Use a spoon to create a design of peaks and valleys all over the meringue. Place in the oven and bake until the meringue is nicely browned, 8 to 10 minutes. Let cool for 15 minutes on a wire rack, then chill at least 1 hour before serving.

Miss Norma's Brown Sugar Chess Pie

When I was a little girl, I was always secretly listening in on my mother's conversations with her lady friends. I was especially intrigued when I'd hear the women say that if a woman knew what was good for her, she'd better learn how to be a lady in the living room, a cook in the kitchen, and a lover in the bedroom. I knew it could be detrimental to a woman's marriage if she incorrectly paired any one those aspects, because I would hear Aunt Marjell talk about a lady named Norma, whose estranged husband was going around town saying that he had left her because she was too much of a lady in the bedroom.

Mama used to say, *Sometimes you have to show another side.*

I didn't know what Miss Norma was doing in her bedroom, but I did know that she was a nice lady in the living room and an excellent cook in the kitchen. And that was good enough for me.

One 9-inch single Flaky Pie Crust (page 8), rolled out, fitted into a pie plate, and edge trimmed and crimped

FILLING

- 1 large egg
- 3 large egg yolks
- 2 cups firmly packed dark brown sugar
- 2 tablespoons all-purpose flour
- 1½ tablespoons fine yellow cornmeal
- ¼ teaspoon salt
- ½ cup (1 stick) unsalted butter, melted
- ¼ cup milk
- ½ teaspoon vanilla extract
- ½ teaspoon red wine vinegar

MERINGUE

- 3 large egg whites, at room temperature
- ¼ teaspoon cream of tartar
- 6 tablespoons granulated sugar
- ½ teaspoon vanilla extract

Makes one 9-inch pie

Preheat the oven to 400 degrees. Prepare the pie crust and set aside.

Make the filling. In a medium-size bowl, combine the whole egg and egg yolks and beat slightly. In another medium-size bowl, combine the brown sugar, flour, cornmeal, and salt, then add to the eggs and stir until smooth. Stir in the melted butter, milk, vanilla, and vinegar until well combined. Pour the filling into the pie crust, place in the oven, and bake for 10 minutes. Reduce the oven temperature to 325 degrees and bake for another 45 minutes. Take the pie out of the oven and increase the oven temperature to 350 degrees.

Meanwhile, make the meringue. In a medium-size bowl, using an electric mixer, beat together the egg whites and cream of tartar until foamy. Add the granulated sugar, 1 tablespoon at a time, beating after each addition, until dissolved. Beat in the vanilla, and beat until shiny, stiff peaks form. Mound in the center of the pie, then spread it evenly around the edge of the inner crust, sealing the meringue to the crust. Use a spoon to create a design of peaks and valleys all over the meringue. Bake until the peaks on the meringue are golden brown, 8 to 10 minutes. Let cool completely on a wire rack.

Odessa Goodlow's Butterscotch Pie with Meringue Topping

When I was a girl, there was a middle-aged woman who lived a few blocks up the street from our house. Her name was Odessa Goodlow and every now and then, as she was passing by, my mother, who enjoyed the company of older women, would invite Miss Goodlow to sit on our front porch.

Most of what my mother and Miss Goodlow talked about was of little interest to me. I knew (from listening in) that Miss Odessa collected African violets and that she liked to pick in her garden. And I knew that she didn't want to be married to her husband, Chester. She would say things like, "The only reason I stay with that ornery man is because I don't have any other way to support myself. Chester is the one with the job and the money. Where am I gonna go with no skills and no money?"

My mother was also a stay-at-home wife. But at age 26, unlike Miss Odessa, my mother entered into her marriage with her own stuff—a bank account and two rent houses. She was always taking night classes—typing, shorthand, sewing, candle making, soap making—to make herself marketable if she ever needed to be. Each time Miss Odessa left, Mama would shake her head. "I pity a woman who doesn't have anything to fall back on," she would say, "'cause I can't see myself having to ask a man for a dollar every time I need a loaf of bread, nor can I see myself staying with a man just for his money."

"Let's go inside," Miss Odessa said to my mother. "I've got a butterscotch pie that I'd like to get your opinion on."

Once, when Mama and I were passing by Miss Odessa's house, she returned Mama's hospitality by inviting us to come onto her porch. Soon as we got there, it became apparent that Miss Odessa couldn't talk the way she wanted to—her broad-shouldered, unsmiling husband was sitting there in a wooden swing, purposefully focused on a section of the newspaper. He appeared too engrossed to acknowledge our arrival with so much as a simple "hello."

"Let's go inside," Miss Odessa said to my mother. "I've got a butterscotch pie that I'd like to get your opinion on." It was Miss Odessa's way of getting Mama inside the house, so that the two of them could talk womanish. Miss Odessa turned to me, "You can sit on the swing next to Chester," she said. "Me 'n' your mama won't be long."

Shortly thereafter, I found my little self sitting arm to arm on the porch swing with Miss Odessa's pot-bellied, grim-faced husband. He had a scowl on his face that looked like it had been pressed on with a hot iron. For me, the atmosphere was tense, much like the wait in a doctor's office. It felt like we were crammed together on that porch swing forever, then, suddenly, the screen door squeaked open and Miss Odessa emerged carrying a tray with two slices of pie on it—a slice for Chester and a slice for me. Miss Odessa placed a napkin under my chin and then one under her husband's. "Now don't you soil your nice little shirt," she said to me. She turned to her husband, "Same goes for you. That shirt's fresh off the line. Don't you go spillin' something on it this early in the day."

I looked up at Miss Odessa's ornery husband. He had a slice of pie in one hand and a sheepish look on his face. I smiled at him, and he smiled back. He had a very nice smile.

From that day forward, whenever Miss Odessa sat on our porch complaining about her husband, telling Mama how cheap and cantankerous he was, and that if she had just one marketable skill she'd take a bus out to California, where her baby sister, Loretta, was living quite well, I would think of her husband's sweet smile and wonder if perhaps Miss Odessa was just one of those disgruntled housewives who are never satisfied, always complaining about something. There are women like that, you know.

One 9-inch single Flaky Pie Crust (page 8), rolled out, fitted into a pie plate, and edge trimmed and crimped

FILLING

1¼ cups firmly packed light brown sugar

¼ cup cornstarch

3 tablespoons all-purpose flour

2 cups whole milk

4 large egg yolks, beaten

½ cup (1 stick) unsalted butter

1 teaspoon vanilla extract

MERINGUE

4 large egg whites, at room temperature

¼ teaspoon cream of tartar

½ cup granulated sugar

½ teaspoon vanilla extract

Makes one 9-inch pie

Preheat the oven to 375 degrees. Prepare the pie crust and fully prebake. Set aside on a wire rack.

Make the filling. Combine the brown sugar, cornstarch, and flour in the top pot of a double boiler. Pour in just enough milk to make a paste. Stir in the egg yolks. Stir in the remainder of the milk. Cook slowly, over boiling water, stirring constantly, until the filling is thick. Remove from the heat. Stir in the butter and vanilla until the butter is melted and thoroughly incorporated. Pour the filling into the pie crust.

Make the meringue. In a medium bowl, using an electric mixer, beat together the egg whites and cream of tartar until foamy. Beat in the sugar, 1 tablespoon at a time, beating well. Add the vanilla and beat until shiny, stiff peaks form. Mound in the center of the pie, then spread it evenly around the edge of the inner crust, sealing the meringue to the crust. Use a spoon to create a design of peaks and valleys all over the meringue. Bake until the peaks in the meringue turn golden brown, 10 to 12 minutes. Let cool completely on a wire rack.

Vertamae Grosvenor's Coconut Custard Meringue Pie

I came from a time when women guarded their precious recipes—the secret potions that seasoned their trademark cornbread, their adored macaroni and cheese, or their acclaimed collard green suppers. From the moment I discovered Vertamae Grosvenor (celebrated cookbook author and culinary anthropologist) in the food section of *Essence* magazine I felt womanishly connected to her. Her meal selections reflected the culinary philosophy that I'd been raised with: a meal doesn't have to be elaborate to be rich. I came of age in the Eartha Kitt era of domesticity, where black women dolled up, switched into their kitchens like cats, and came out purring, bearing sensual dinners encased in seasoned soup pots and black skillets. Reading Vertamae and collecting her luscious recipes, took me back to that time, back to soul food school. Those were the times when Mama, who was teaching me how to prepare good suppers, would call me into the kitchen at various stages of her cooking, and say, almost in the manner of someone who was sharing a secret, "I want you to see how I do this . . ."

Years after reading Miss Vertamae's food stories and collecting her recipes, I had the pleasure of meeting the first lady of womanish cooking: she and I were guests on NPR's Roundtable with Ed Gordon. We kept in touch, and now, from time to time, we talk on the phone about cooking and recipes as if we'd known each other our entire lives.

One 9-inch single Flaky Pie Crust (page 8), rolled out, fitted into a pie plate, and edge trimmed and crimped

FILLING

1 cup sugar

¼ cup cornstarch

¼ teaspoon salt

3 cups whole milk

3 large egg yolks

1 cup sweetened shredded coconut

½ teaspoon coconut extract

½ teaspoon vanilla extract

2 tablespoons unsalted butter

MERINGUE

3 large egg whites, at room temperature

½ teaspoon cream of tartar

3 tablespoons sugar

¾ teaspoon cornstarch

¼ cup sweetened shredded coconut

Makes one 9-inch pie

Preheat the oven to 350 degrees. Prepare the pie crust and fully prebake. Set aside on a wire rack.

Make the filling. In a large, heavy saucepan, combine the sugar, cornstarch, and salt. Gradually whisk in the milk until well blended. Cook over medium heat, whisking constantly, until the mixture thickens and begins to boil. Remove from the heat.

In a medium-size bowl, beat the egg yolks until thick and lemon colored. Slowly stir about ¼ cup of the hot milk mixture into the beaten egg yolks. Pour the egg yolk mixture into the saucepan. Cook over medium heat for 1 minute, stirring constantly. Remove from the heat and stir in the coconut, extracts, and butter until the butter melts and is thoroughly incorporated. Pour the filling into the pie crust.

Make the meringue. In a large bowl, using an electric mixer, beat together the egg whites and cream of tartar until foamy. Gradually beat in the sugar, 1 tablespoon at a time, and the cornstarch, beating well after each addition. Continue to beat until shiny, stiff peaks form. Mound the meringue in the center of the pie, then spread it evenly around the edge of the inner crust, sealing the meringue to the crust. Use a spoon to create a design of peaks and valleys all over the meringue. Sprinkle the coconut evenly over the meringue. Place in the oven and bake until the meringue is a luscious golden brown and the coconut is toasted, 8 to 10 minutes. Let cool completely on a wire rack before serving.

Index

Rhubarb + Strawberry Pie

2½ c. diced rhubarb
1½ c. hulled strawberries
2 T. quick cooking tapioca
Few grains salt
1½ c. sugar

Mix ingredients; fill pastry-lined 9" pie ... with pastry; make ... slits f... Bake ... Reduce ... bakin...

Butter-Scotch Pie

1 c. brown sugar
1½ c. milk
2 T. butter
2 T. flour
2 eggs
1 tsp vanilla
¼ tsp. salt

Mix brown sugar, flour, and salt. Add milk and egg yolks. Cook until thickened. Add butter and vanilla.

Rhubarb + Strawberry Pie

diced rhubarb
hulled strawberries

2 T. quick cooking tapioca
Few grains salt
1 1/2 c. sugar

...ix ingredients; fill pastry-lined pie tin. Cover with pastry; make ...ts for ste... vents. ...ake in ve... ...50° for 10 min ...duce hea... ...king fo...

Butter-Scotch Pie

1 c. brown sugar
1 1/2 c. milk
2 T. butter

2 T. flour
2 eggs
1 tsp vanilla
1/4 tsp. salt

Mix brown sugar, flour, and salt. Add milk and egg yolks. Cook until thickened. Add butter and vanilla.